STRESS-TEST YOUR
RETIREMENT

STRESS-TEST YOUR
RETIREMENT

CREATE A PLAN FOR AN
EVER-CHANGING ECONOMY

MATT GULBRANSEN

Published by Advantage, Charleston, South Carolina.
Member of Advantage Media Group.

ADVANTAGE is a registered trademark, and the Advantage colophon is a trademark of Advantage Media Group, Inc.

Printed in the United States of America.

ISBN: 978-1-59932-775-4
LCCN: 2016959622

Cover design by Katie Biondo.

This publication is designed to provide accurate and authoritative information in regard to the subject matter covered. It is sold with the understanding that the publisher is not engaged in rendering legal, accounting, or other professional services. If legal advice or other expert assistance is required, the services of a competent professional person should be sought.

Advantage Media Group is proud to be a part of the Tree Neutral® program. Tree Neutral offsets the number of trees consumed in the production and printing of this book by taking proactive steps such as planting trees in direct proportion to the number of trees used to print books. To learn more about Tree Neutral, please visit **www.treeneutral.com.**

Advantage Media Group is a publisher of business, self-improvement, and professional development books. We help entrepreneurs, business leaders, and professionals share their Stories, Passion, and Knowledge to help others Learn & Grow. Do you have a manuscript or book idea that you would like us to consider for publishing? Please visit **advantagefamily.com** or call **1.866.775.1696.**

*To my loving family for all the encouragement
and support as I pursue my dreams.*

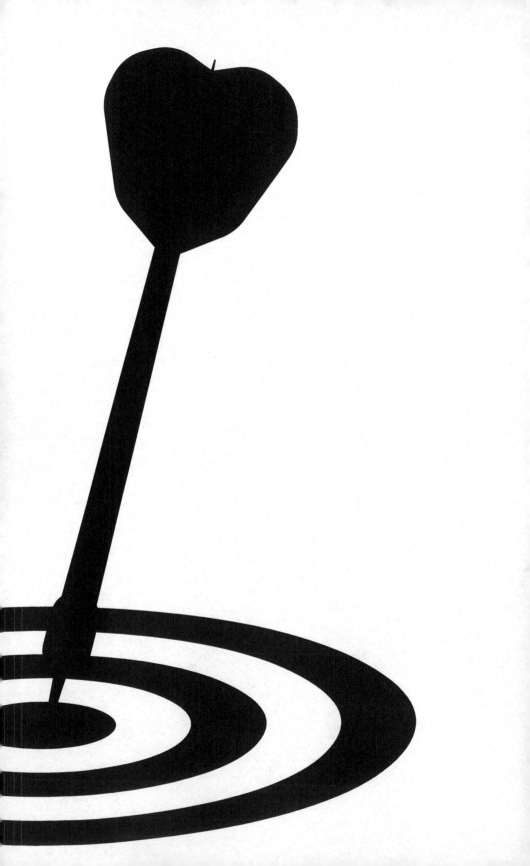

TABLE OF CONTENTS

All anecdotes shared in this book are based on actual, direct experience with clients. Details have been adjusted for privacy purposes.

A FARM KID'S STORY

I was born and raised on a family farm in southern Minnesota. By necessity, farmers are probably some of the best planners you'll ever meet. They have to be; farming, from one season to the next, is unpredictable.

Growing up, I witnessed a variety of short-, mid-, and long-range planning. My parents made conservative assumptions and carefully considered every possible scenario. Due to the unpredictable nature of their business, they did not want to rely to heavily on outcomes they could not count on, nor did they want to take on too much risk.

The lessons I learned as a kid about planning were a big motivator in what I do today. They are why I take a comprehensive approach to helping people prepare their financial plans for retirement.

My parents also taught me about money from an early age. I was a fortunate "farm kid" because I was actually paid for my work. Family farms are family projects; everybody's expected to do their share. Our work provided the necessities of life: good food on the table, a sound roof over our heads, and clothes on our backs. But my parents also realized that if my efforts didn't earn something that was "just mine" as well, I might not fully appreciate the value of hard work.

That wisdom is another big factor in why I do what I do.

If you are serious about putting together a comprehensive financial plan for retirement—and I hope you are because the way we retire today is very different and far more dependent on personal savings than ever before—this book can help. It's based on a course I've developed and taught in continuing education programs at local school districts and community colleges for several years.

Between that course and my practice, Callahan Financial Planning, I've helped hundreds of people create effective personal financial plans for retirement. This book can teach you the keys to doing so, as well.

The better you understand something, the more likely you are not just to stick with it but also to have confidence in what you're doing. It's difficult to overstate the importance of confidence when planning for retirement. It's not only knowing what you're doing, but why, that is the key. I believe the information, client experiences, and level of detail shared here will provide the critical knowledge and motivation you need to take action.

And action, of course, is crucial. Procrastination is one of the biggest reasons people fail to create a financial plan for retirement, despite knowing they should.

Though this book provides a wealth of solid information, there are a couple of things it won't give you.

First of all, there's no sales pitch. I'm not going to talk about specific products, because at this point, products really don't matter. The object here is not to sell you something. It's to help you figure out where you are now and where you want to go. Without a clear understanding of those two things, it's impossible to determine appropriate solutions, let alone specific products that might help you reach your goals.

Something else you won't find here is a magic formula, some crazy-simple financial equation or ratio that, if followed, will guarantee you the retirement of your dreams—because there's no such thing. Every one of my clients, all the people who have attended my courses, and everyone who reads this book has different goals, needs, lifestyles, asset levels, risk tolerances, housing costs, medical expenses, and life expectancies.

Nonetheless, we see one-size-fits-all "retirement formulas" all the time—on the Internet, in magazines, and on TV. Each of them has one thing in common: They're absurd. If everyone has different needs, goals, and expectations, how can any one formula work? You need to customize this stuff to your specific, personal situation. Without doing that work—or better yet, getting a professional's help with the work that must be done—you can't even begin to know what options might work best for you.

Even when you have committed to a plan and begun to implement it, however, you're still not finished. As the book's title suggests, you need to run stress tests. Just as my parents did in planning the farm's production, you need to put your plan through every scenario, every possible eventuality that might affect it—because things change over time.

The book is presented in two parts and is designed to help anyone who is serious about taking sequential steps toward securing their financial future.

Part one eases you into the process. The first chapter clearly establishes the importance of creating a financial plan. I share the philosophy I take in helping clients, along with the formative experiences that led me to do this work. In chapter 2, the focus shifts to where it remains the rest of the way: on you. We begin by defining your retirement goals and desires and then turn to your financials—present and future—in chapters 3 and 4, respectively.

In part two the heavy lifting begins, as we study options for establishing, growing, and ultimately drawing on your retirement savings. Upon finishing chapter 5, you'll know far more about the various options for building your savings—and about how those options work—than you do right now. You'll also, very probably, be surprised by the number of options available.

Chapter 6 takes the mystery out of investing, exploring in great detail the hows and whys of poor investment decisions. It then points to strategies, borne out by the history of the financial markets, that can help your retirement savings grow.

In chapter 7, I share ideas for distributing your retirement savings among three "buckets," whose contents are typically taxed at different rates. This can help reduce your overall tax liability, which is the surest way of increasing the income available from your retirement assets.

Protecting those assets is critical, too, and chapter 8 details several insurance tools that can help you do just that. We finish with a consideration for estate planning in chapter 9, and the conclusion offers ideas for finding trusted help in formulating and implementing your retirement plan.

Along the way, with solid information, client stories, and hopefully a smile or two, you'll uncover what your retirement can and should be: a vibrant new chapter of life, brimming with activity, opportunity—and, yes, relaxation. Thank you for extending me the privilege of helping to chart your course.

PART ONE

CHARTING YOUR COURSE TO RETIREMENT

CHAPTER 1

WHY YOU NEED A FINANCIAL PLAN FOR RETIREMENT

"By failing to plan, you are planning to fail."

This quote attributed to Benjamin Franklin is one of my favorites.

That's probably not surprising coming from a guy who believes making a financial plan for retirement is probably the most important thing you can do.

Besides being one of our nation's founders and helping to write the Declaration of Independence, Ben Franklin was all about thinking ahead. He knew life's unexpected surprises don't need to be unexpected at all. Better, Franklin believed, to be ready for anything.

His quote about planning is so well known that most people don't realize what he actually wrote: "By failing to *prepare*, you are *preparing* to fail."

That's even more powerful, isn't it? By simply proceeding through life unprepared for whatever might come your way, you are *preparing* to fail.

Franklin is rightly recognized as one of the smartest people of his time—and since—but I never understood the depth of his wisdom until I started writing this book. Despite being published more than two hundred and fifty years ago, most of Franklin's ideas are more vital now than ever. I'll share a few more of his ideas over the next several chapters, but for now, let's look more closely at this one.

Franklin is saying that instead of thinking ahead and considering what might happen, we tend to go about our busy lives and trust that things will work out in the end. Even though we know it's smart to have a plan that will help us weather bad times and capitalize on good times, few of us do. Instead of anticipating every possibility, we comfort ourselves when something bad happens with a familiar excuse: "It was totally *unexpected*!"

That's about as far as you can get from *preparing*, isn't it?

At least we do a better job of planning for the things we expect to happen. Don't we?

Surprisingly, no. It should be a no-brainer, but few of us plan for those things, either!

Retirement is the perfect example. We know it's coming. Many people—especially where I'm from, Minnesota—have headed out the door thinking, *I'll be glad when I can stop getting up in the dead of winter to do this! One of these days I'll be rolling over in bed while everyone else is shoveling their driveway so they can get to work!*

We know retirement is on the way. We expect it to happen. But research shows we do little or nothing to prepare.

Even scarier, many of us will retire sooner than we think.

The Employee Benefit Research Institute (EBRI), a nonprofit, nonpartisan group that tracks such things, says just one in four of us expects to stop working full time before we reach age sixty-five—but in reality, *two out of three* leave the workforce before that "traditional" retirement age.

Think about that, about what it really looks like. Imagine you're in a room with nineteen other people. Only five of you think you'll retire by sixty-five. In fact, thirteen of you will!

EBRI also has some sobering information about how we plan for retirement—or more accurately, how we *don't*. Take a look at this chart. It shows the percentage of time we devote to planning for various events in a typical year.

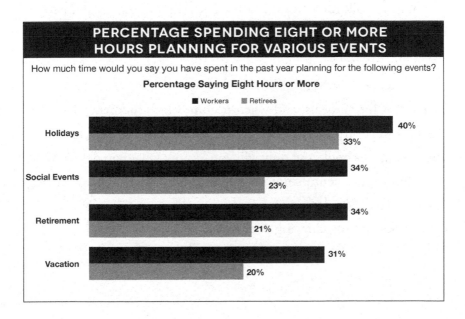

PERCENTAGE SPENDING EIGHT OR MORE HOURS PLANNING FOR VARIOUS EVENTS

How much time would you say you have spent in the past year planning for the following events?

Percentage Saying Eight Hours or More

■ Workers　■ Retirees

Event	Workers	Retirees
Holidays	40%	33%
Social Events	34%	23%
Retirement	34%	21%
Vacation	31%	20%

Pretty amazing, right? We spend as much time planning for holidays, social events, and vacations as we do planning for retirement. And the news gets worse.

According to a study released by the Government Accountability Office in 2015, 41 percent of US households in the fifty-five to sixty-four age group have *no retirement savings*—at all[1]. How sad is *that*?

To recap: We're generally failing to plan for the future—and there's a better than fifty-fifty chance that future—our retirement—will arrive sooner we think! Talk about a double-whammy.

Not to worry. Even if you're not thinking about your retirement, I am. That's why I wrote this book.

I'm the owner of Callahan Financial Planning, serving clients in the Minneapolis-St. Paul metro area. I also teach a personal enrichment course on retirement planning at local school districts and community colleges. Over the years, I've helped hundreds of people learn the keys to planning successfully for retirement. This book is based on my course.

Someone once said, "We don't know what we don't know." That's true for all of us, and when it comes to retirement planning, most people don't know where to start. But I promise you this: After you've read this book, not only will you "know what you don't know" now about retirement planning, but you will also know how putting together a flexible plan, customized to your unique situation, is critically important to achieving your retirement goals.

1 United States Government Accountability Office, "Most Households Approaching Retirement Have Low Savings," May 2015, http://www.gao.gov/assets/680/670153.pdf.

THE MYTH OF A "MAGIC FORMULA"

When I first got into this industry, I noticed lot of things I didn't like. Above all, it seemed like most people were just running around selling products. To me, that's like a doctor asking you what's wrong and writing a prescription before you've finished answering. As far as I'm concerned, that's malpractice.

We're not going to talk about specific products anywhere in this book, because at this point, products are irrelevant. Your top priority should be to understand where you are now, to diagnose your current condition. Only then can you start thinking about the solution—the prescription—that's right for you.

Did I just say *the* solution? Because this is important, too: there is no magic formula, no "A + B = a happy retirement." I can't stress that enough. The key to successful planning is that your plan be flexible, adaptable enough to changing conditions that the overall goal remains achievable. To throw out some sort of one-size-fits-all formula, or to think we can just plug in a couple of variables and get the answers we need—well, that's ludicrous.

I know they're out there, too. In the financial media, on the Internet, wherever—there are these crazy "simple retirement planning guidelines." For example, to retire comfortably, you:

- must save eight times your current income.
- need a million dollars. Better yet, two million.
- will never run out of money if you only take 5 percent per year from your retirement savings.
- should become a more conservative investor in retirement.

Each of these, on its own, is absurd. They may not work. In my opinion, anyone who says they will, without further diagnosis, is committing *financial* malpractice.

Everyone who reads this book will have different goals, lifestyles, medical needs, income and asset levels, risk tolerances, and life expectancies. That means one person's "A" and "B" are going to be completely different from someone else's.

Put simply, one size does *not* fit all.

Your retirement plan must be customized to your specific, personal situation—and nobody knows that situation better than you. Doing the work yourself—or even better, with the help of a trusted, experienced advisor—is the only way to get a thorough understanding of all your options.

Even then, you're not done. You need to "stress-test" your plan.

By that, I mean you must run it through a host of scenarios and look at options that will allow it to adapt when "the unexpected" occurs.

STRESS-TESTING LIKE "THE FED"

We have all heard of the Federal Reserve, which controls monetary policy for our country. "The Fed," as it is known, runs the most detailed, precise stress-testing imaginable before it applies various tools to help steer the nation's economic course. More importantly, the Fed continually adjusts its plan as variables require.

The tool we hear the most about is raising and lowering interest rates. The Fed stress-tests the effects of adjusting rates based on thousands of variables, to see how their action might impact the economy: What if unemployment goes up or down? What if gross domestic product heads in this or that direction? What would result from the combination of such events and whatever action The Fed is considering on interest rates?

The Fed wrestles with such questions constantly in trying to determine whether the policies in place now or the changes it might make will have positive or negative effects. On top of that, it weighs whether the economy will benefit more, over the longer term, from a seemingly "positive" or "negative" impact in the near term. It all seems mind-boggling, but the Fed does it.

Shouldn't you take the same care with your retirement?

Stress-testing your investment portfolio to see how it will react to changing life circumstances makes obvious sense. For example, you can plan based on living to a given age—but what if you live longer? How would that affect your cash flow, and what steps can you take to help cover yourself?

Doesn't it also make sense to pinpoint the right time to take a pension or Social Security and to optimize these together so your retirement income flows as efficiently as possible?

And what about taxes? What's the best strategy for keeping them at a minimum, once you've retired and every dollar counts?

These are not questions to be taken lightly. Again, we know retirement is coming! Do you really want to rely on hope or on some "magic" formula?

Retirement planning isn't a one-time project. It's a habit that must be developed, and that's just what this book will help you do—develop the habit of looking out for your own future.

MY STORY

Before we dig in, though, you might be wondering, *Why is this guy so passionate about financial planning?* Why does he care so much about something that, based on his own numbers, many of us ignore or avoid until it's too late?

As I mentioned, I grew up on a family farm. Like all farm kids, I had chores to do that helped with the operation—but unlike a lot of other farm parents, mine paid me for my work. They were teaching me how to be a saver and how money works.

By a pretty young age, I'd saved up a few thousand dollars. Back then, bank savings accounts were paying 4 or 5 percent interest, which sounds amazing by current standards, but everything's relative. Interest rates were considerably higher on everything, so it wasn't much—and I got curious. If a super-safe bank will pay me 4 percent, could I take more risk but potentially make more money? I was at least smart enough to ask, at a pretty young age.

So, my parents took me to a stockbroker. He said a whole bunch of stuff, and I really had no clue what he was talking about. But I was intrigued by the idea of investing, so I nodded my head while he talked, and Dad gave me the okay to buy my first mutual fund.

This was the early to mid 1990s, and that first investment was the Alliance Bernstein Information Technology fund. If you were investing back then, you can probably guess where this is going.

It was the early days of the Internet. Silicon Valley was booming. Companies were going public every day of the week, whether they had the underlying financials to justify it or not. Tech stocks were red hot; everybody wanted them. These companies—though they had no idea where profits would come from or if they would come at all—became the darlings of Wall Street, and stockbrokers like mine pushed them hard.

The now-infamous "tech bubble" had begun to inflate.

I was just a kid. I didn't know anything about that, only that my $3,000 was growing very, very quickly. Soon, it had more than doubled. By the time I went off to college, I'd stopped paying any attention to that account. Being a typical teenager, I had "more important" things on my mind.

Like sports.

And girls.

Mainly, sports.

Besides, I was clearly a financial wizard! Money? That's easy! You just put it in there and it grows, right?

At least I had the excuse of youthful inexperience. Many more-seasoned investors didn't understand what was happening either—or more likely, didn't want to. And many faced financial ruin when the bubble finally burst.

Though I'd stopped paying attention, Mom had my back. One day, she called me at college to check in. "The stock market has been going down recently," she said. "When you come home at break, you should really take a look at your statement."

I did—and my jaw dropped. My $3,000 stake, which had become almost $7,000 (the last time I looked), had plummeted to around $4,500! I was barely profitable from my initial investment!

That really got me thinking, *Why didn't the stockbroker call me? How did he not see this coming? What do these guys really do all day long? Do they just sit around and buy and sell stocks? How does all this work?*

I did some deep research—serious enough that, the next thing I knew, I was interviewing for internships at financial firms.

I was nineteen years old, still in college, and one of Merrill Lynch's youngest interns. What I saw in a couple years of working there—and I'm just being honest—I really didn't like. It seemed like it was a lot of people just pushing products, trying to generate commissions.

When I took my first paid job at Morgan Stanley, it was more of the same. They continuously pushed their own products and platforms, going after big investors—and charging big fees.

These experiences were a real awakening. They led me to where I am today and are why I'm so passionate about helping people to plan for the future.

I'm not interested in pushing products. I want to help people see the bigger picture. With knowledge of all the tools available—and with careful planning based on their unique situations—they can enjoy the kind of retirement they really want to have.

That's what my firm is all about. We take a holistic approach to creating flexible financial plans that help protect and grow our clients' assets.

MY PLANNING PHILOSOPHY

"Holistic." It's a term often associated with medicine, and that's twice now I've referenced the medical world. Earlier, I equated selling people a financial product for retirement without understanding their situation to a doctor committing malpractice. I really believe that's true.

The way we get medical services and the way we should think about planning for retirement have a lot in common, as the following illustration shows. Start at step one and follow it clockwise.

MEDICAL TREATMENT VS. RETIREMENT PLANNING

If you are feeling sick, you may follow these steps to receive medical care.

1. You're not feeling well, so you go to your doctor's office. He asks a lot of questions about how you feel and what's happening.

2. You're put through a set of diagnostics tests to analyze your symptoms.

3. The doc studies the test results and considers possible diagnoses. Things are narrowed down. Your doctor now has a good idea of what's ailing you, but must be sure.

4. He digs even deeper. More questions. More tests. Perhaps he brings in a specialist.

5. Finally, it's time for diagnosis and treatment. Your doc might prescribe rest, medicine, surgery, physical therapy, or some combination of these. But it doesn't end there.

6. A good doctor, whether weeks or months later, will bring you back to be sure that his prescribed treatment worked and that no new issues have surfaced. And next year, you'll see him again.

I follow these same steps with my patients—oops, clients!—in putting together their retirement plans.

1. When do you want to retire? Do you have any specific goals for your future? What are you most concerned about? Have you had any traumatic experiences with investing in the past?

Do you need a certain amount of money to live on? What is your tolerance for risk?

2. What does retirement look like for you? What are your current assets and obligations? What are the chances you'll retire sooner—or later—than you think? How do you plan to spend all the free time you're going to have? Where do you want to live? Will you be a "snowbird," heading for Florida for other points south in the winter to play golf or tennis? Or maybe your dream retirement is traveling the world. Or fishing every day.

3. We must answer those questions before devising a plan and doing stress-tests for all the variables that will—or might— come into play. I've already mentioned a few: goals, lifestyle, medical needs, income and asset levels, risk tolerance, life expectancy. There is another I haven't mentioned yet, and it's the most important: the income gap. (We'll learn about it in chapter 3.)

4. We model for inflation, the investment environment, taxes, even cognitive decline—something most of us don't like to think about but which often comes with getting older.

5. After we've "diagnosed" your current status, figured out where you want to go, and looked at all the variables, we're ready for a "prescription"—your retirement plan.

6. Most important, regular "checkups" to see if the prescription is working. Is your plan holding up compared to how things are actually playing out? Maybe your income significantly increased—or declined. Are the other variables on track or maybe running a little higher? Or lower? Even seemingly small amounts can make a big difference over a twenty- or thirty-year period, so we pinpoint them—and adjust your plan to keep you on course. Every year or so, we do it all again, just like a good doctor.

YOUR BIGGEST ENEMY? YOURSELF

Maybe you've heard of David McClelland. Unless you study human motivation, I doubt it. But what he discovered drives my work and has convinced me that careful planning is the key to success.

Dr. McClelland taught psychology at Harvard. He studied business owners and entrepreneurs to define the traits that set them apart. One thing really stood out: Those who were more successful had highly detailed business plans.

How that translates to retirement is easy to see. We must treat our personal finances like a business. We must have a detailed plan in place.

There's really no excuse, no good reason, for any of us to "wing it" into retirement, but—as we've seen in this chapter—we do, thanks to what I believe Ben Franklin would have considered the worst habit of all: procrastination. We simply put it off—and many of us keep putting it off until it's too late.

Dr. McClelland's research proved that people who take action, who really understand the value of planning and see their plans through, do dramatically better than those who delay until the absolute last moment. It's as simple as that.

So don't delay. To take step one toward the retirement you want, just turn the page.

CHAPTER 2

YOUR FUTURE: RETIREMENT GOALS AND DESIRES

"If passion drives you, let reason hold the reins."

The wisdom in this quote from ol' Ben is obvious: Passion that is not rooted in reason is dangerous.

Nowhere is this more true than when you're planning for retirement.

Every department in every company has at least one of them—that employee who yearns to retire early. Most have a clear vision, something they want to do—often it's something physically demanding, which they stand a much better chance of accomplishing at age fifty-five or sixty than they would ten years later.

Some of these early retirees, however, have one objective only: Not to work at all, toward any objective.

As we're about to see, a passion for doing nothing can be dangerous indeed.

GARY'S STORY

Throughout his working life, Gary had one goal—to make as much money as possible, save all he could, and retire early, just like his dad.

Gary didn't think much about what he'd do in retirement, because he never made time to think about it, let alone to discover what his passions might be. He was committed to working like crazy until he turned sixty and then . . . just . . . stopping.

After working his way through the ranks at several other companies, Gary spent the last fifteen years of his career overseeing the IT department at a leading medical device company. He was charged with integrating, maintaining, and constantly upgrading the company's tech infrastructure and functionality.

Gary did his job well. He earned incentive bonuses for bringing projects to successful completion. Some paid in cash but most in the form of company stock. He worked sixty hours or more most weeks and spent his all-too-short weekends catching up on sleep, recharging for the next week's marathon.

Gary's dad happily lived off his pension after working for the same company all his life. Though he didn't have a pension, Gary figured he'd be fine. He had paid off his house and put what seemed like a lot of money into his 401(k), most of it, like bonuses he received, in company stock.

What did he do for fun?

In a word, nothing.

Unlike his dad, who was an avid golfer and traveler, Gary had no hobbies or interests outside of work. His failure to limit his work hours to something more reasonable prevented him from discovering a non-work passion, or life purpose, that he could pursue in retirement.

He worked such long hours that his sole focus was escaping the daily grind. He'd often tell coworkers that his dream retirement was doing "absolutely nothing."

Gary followed his dream, and it quickly became a nightmare.

In less than a year of doing nothing every day, Gary realized that a happy retirement requires defined objectives and a plan for reaching them, two things he'd never bothered with. If he had, his financial picture might have been as rosy as he'd imagined.

The cost of health insurance especially surprised him. By retiring at sixty, Gary needed to fill a five-year gap in coverage until becoming eligible for Medicare. Quickly escalating premiums put a much bigger dent in his 401(k) than he'd imagined.

To make matters worse, holding so much company stock proved costly as well, in the form of a larger tax liability than he expected.

Gary's biggest mistake, however, was thinking his retirement would "just work out," like his dad's. Huge changes in how we retire—changes Gary never even considered—pretty much assured that wouldn't be the case.

RETIREMENT AS IT USED TO BE

Back when your parents or grandparents were working, most people worked at the same company for most of their careers. That was really how pensions get started. Since people didn't want to give up their pensions, they worked for the same employer, many for thirty or forty years, like Gary's dad.

And what, you might ask, is a pension? If you're not sure, you're not alone. Pensions are quickly becoming a thing of the past.

Classified as "defined benefit plans," pensions, throughout much of the last century, were the backbone of American retirement. For decades, large corporations and private companies retained employees by offering pensions. Here's how they worked.

Employers told each employee, *up front*, how much money they—the *employer!*—would pay them annually, beginning at a specific future date, in return for their long-term commitment as an employee. That payout was the "defined benefit" and was based on the "defined benefit period"—the length of service to which the employee agreed in advance.

At the end of that period—ten, fifteen, twenty, twenty-five years, or more—workers got the money the company had socked away for them in the form of an annuity, a guaranteed annual income in retirement. No wonder pension plans helped companies keep workers, right? They were a real incentive for staying!

For many people who have entered the workforce in the past thirty years or so, pensions seem beyond belief. Few companies offer them these days, but as recently as 1975, 88 percent of private-sector firms did, according to the National Institute on Retirement Security.

Why have pensions gone away?

It depends who you ask. Most analysts agree that the decline in pensions is tied to profound changes in the nature of work itself. Some consider pensions "golden handcuffs" for middle-class Americans, keeping them tied to the same company for years and years.

Of course, that thinking cuts both ways. Pensions handcuff employers, too.

Companies often underfunded their pension plans, believing the markets would perform better than they did. When that performance didn't materialize, the company was still "on the hook" for the promised amount of the defined benefit.

During the economic bonanza of the post-World War II era, many companies gladly made the payout to ensure worker loyalty—but those days are gone.

Today, corporate profits are higher than ever, but Wall Street's demands for consistent, predictably competitive earnings have forced companies to get their numbers and projections as precise as possible. Variables like market volatility and life expectancy of employees simply loom too large in those calculations, and that reality has forced most companies to abandon or freeze pension plans. By 2013, just 18 percent of private-sector firms offered them, according to the Bureau of Labor Statistics.[2]

Compare that to the 88 percent that offered pensions a generation ago, and it's easy to understand why I'm seeing fewer clients who have worked for the same company for more than twenty or twenty-five years. The baby boom generation is really the last to see that kind of long-term commitment to a single employer, and it's a pretty safe bet that the current generation of workers won't see pension plans making a comeback anytime soon.

Besides the disappearance of pensions, two other changes have roiled retirement in recent decades: longer life expectancies and the fact that people are retiring earlier than ever before. Together, these

---

2 "The last private industry pension plans," January 3, 2013, Bureau of Labor Statistics, http://www.bls.gov/opub/ted/2013/ted_20130103.htm.

have diminished the value of another key retirement benefit that prior generations relied on: Social Security.

Social Security was established in an era where workers would devote their lives to one company and work until age sixty-five, maybe a little longer. Then they would take that nice pension we just talked about and, with a little luck, enjoy ten or twelve years of leisure before passing on. Social Security was the icing on the cake; it provided the remaining income folks needed in order to fully enjoy their "golden years."

Prior generations didn't have a unique vision of how they wanted to spend their retirements; they really didn't need one. People worked later in life and life expectancies were shorter. With only ten or twelve years in retirement, minimal financial planning was enough.

We, on the other hand, can expect twenty, thirty, or more years of retirement. While this gives us opportunities our parents never had, it also makes careful planning absolutely crucial.

HOW WE RETIRE NOW

Today, we are far more responsible for our retirement's success and for creating the income to pay for it. Not only do one-quarter of us hope to retire before we reach age sixty-five, but as we learned in chapter 1, many more of us actually will: *nearly two-thirds!*

One reason is that companies are offering incentives for older workers to step aside early and make room for younger, lower-cost employees. Another factor is changes in how we are employed. A growing number of industries are trending away from hiring full-time workers in favor of part-timers, flex-timers, and subcontractors to avoid providing benefits. Chronic medical conditions are yet another reason we might retire earlier than we think.

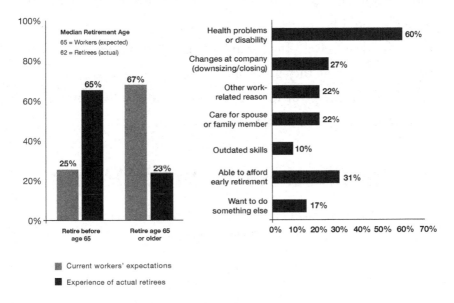

Current expectations of retirement vs. actual experience of retirees

Reasons cited for retiring earlier than planned

Meanwhile, life expectancies are going up across the board. People living into their nineties are now the fastest-growing age group in our country.[3]

None of these factors were an issue for our parents and grandparents, as we saw in the last section. For them, the combination of pensions, Social Security, and shorter life expectancies made retirement manageable.

Today, company-funded pensions—those "defined benefit plans" we just discussed—have become "defined contribution plans," the 401(k), 403(b), and 457-type plans to which many of us contribute part of our pre-tax earnings. Today's workers count heavily on such plans to help fund their retirements.

3 "Census Bureau Releases Comprehensive Analysis of Fast-Growing 90-and-Older Population" United States Census Bureau, November 17, 2011, http://www.census.gov/newsroom/releases/archives/aging_population/cb11-194.html.

This is a fundamental shift. In a single generation, we've gone from employers telling us what our payout—from plans *they funded*—would be, to telling us what they will chip in to plans we mostly fund ourselves. The company's match or profit-sharing contribution (assuming they make one) is nice, and we're foolish if we're not taking advantage of it. But the responsibility for funding our retirements has shifted almost entirely onto us.

Qualified Retirement Plans

Participating in retirement benefits by type of plan[1]
(all private industry)

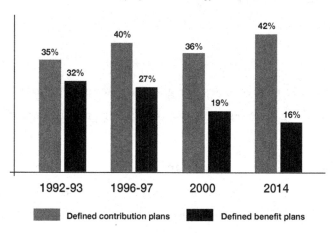

1992-93   1996-97   2000   2014

Defined contribution plans   Defined benefit plans

[1]Bureau of Labor Statistics, National Compensation Survey—Benefits

To formulate a plan that ensures you won't run out of money in retirement, you first need to know what you want retirement to look like. Getting a clear vision of your retirement is what the rest of this chapter is all about.

PICTURING YOUR RETIREMENT

A happy retirement really comes down to just a few things.

First and foremost is your own comfort, having confidence in what you're doing, knowing that you have a viable action plan that accounts for all the risks and "bumps in the road" that could arise during retirement. The more confident you are in your plan, the more likely you are to stick with it.

Secondly—and this has nothing to the do with finances—you need to figure out how you're going to fill your time in retirement. You're going to have a lot more of it than ever before. Every day is Saturday! You don't want to just sit inside your house and watch TV all day. Or maybe you do—but I'm hoping you want to get out, be around other people, and have fun. That means having what Gary, who we met earlier in this chapter, did not: a purpose.

On the flipside of that, too often I see people remain active for a year or two after retiring but then increasingly isolate themselves— sometimes without even realizing it.

Just as putting together a financial plan takes effort, so too does staying active in retirement. The clearer your picture of retirement, the better your chances of living it. You need to think deeply about what will make you happiest. What do you want to do, to see? How will you spend the abundance of time you will have?

It's not entirely about money, but money is certainly a key factor of any good retirement plan. You don't necessarily need a huge nest egg. In fact, some studies show that people with regular, predict- able income during retirement—from sources like Social Security, pensions, guaranteed annuities—are happier than those with a huge chunk of money. But however you plan to derive retirement income, you first need to sit down with your family or spouse and develop that clear picture. What will be your purpose in retirement?

The financial decisions become much, much easier once you know where you want to go.

As this chapter has shown, the burden for funding retirement has shifted. Employers once provided generous pensions in exchange for long-term worker loyalty. Today, workers must set aside the money that will secure their financial futures.

We've also learned that the current crop of retirees wants more. Many expect to retire younger than prior generations, and they're getting what they want, thanks to the changing realities of work.

Last, and perhaps most critically, we're living longer than ever before. This means we'll be spending more time in retirement than the generations that preceded us.

All these realities make careful retirement planning a must, not an option. Putting together a flexible, adaptive plan requires serious thought about what we want to achieve when our full-time careers have ended.

HOMEWORK: DEFINING YOUR IDEAL RETIREMENT

The questions that follow will help you determine your purpose in retirement.

Some people find it helpful to take several days to think things over. Many different interests capture our imaginations throughout our lives; it can be hard to remember them all in one sitting. Sorting out those that might hold your attention in retirement takes real reflection.

Maybe you want to learn to play golf. Maybe you're a scratch golfer already, and playing a round each morning is your idea of the perfect retirement.

Perhaps you've always admired beautiful quilts and want to create your own, to be enjoyed for generations to come.

Or maybe you've always wanted to help others, and retirement is the time you've set aside for doing so. But where to focus your efforts—in your neighborhood, your city, your state, or in some other country?

Wherever your interests may lie, thinking seriously about the following questions will help you unearth them and prioritize their importance during retirement. If, as you work, you find yourself wondering where the money will come from, remember, that's the best reason for committing to formulate a financial plan! But for now, focus on creating a clear picture of the retirement you want to live. Then we'll work toward a plan to get you there.

Let's get to it!

QUESTIONS FOR PLANNING FOR RETIREMENT

1. How do you currently spend your weekends? Could you envision yourself doing that most days?

2. Do you have any hobbies that could take up significant amounts of time? Would these hobbies incorporate a spouse or friend?

3. Is volunteering important to you?

4. Do you have a vision for travel or spending part of the year in a different climate?

5. Dedicating time to family is important. Do you see yourself filling free time with family more than in the past?

6. Most people's career required a lot of responsibility and they were heavily relied on. Now that you are retired, are you going to miss the feeling of being depended on?

7. Imagine it is Tuesday afternoon and you are now retired. What comes to mind when you think about what you would be spending your time doing?

8. Is learning or acquiring a new talent or hobby something you will pursue?

CHAPTER 3

THE ELEPHANT IN THE ROOM: YOUR INCOME GAP

"A penny saved is two pence clear."

Y ou always thought Ben Franklin said, "A penny saved is a penny earned," didn't you? Not quite.

So, what does he mean? And what's "two pence" anyway?

"Pence" is the plural of "penny," although today, here in America at least, we say "pennies" instead. (The Brits still use "pence.") Franklin first wrote this often-misquoted line in 1737, in a column titled, "Hints For Those Who Would Be Rich."

To say Ben Franklin was "thrifty" is an understatement. Franklin believed that creating personal wealth had as much to do with being fiscally prudent as with being a shrewd investor. If we can resist spending a penny, his reasoning went, we are actually two pennies ahead of those who can't resist, who give in to temptation and spend money on something they don't need—especially if they're spending on credit.

Let's think about that in modern terms.

A penny from Franklin's time is worth forty-three pence today—so a dollar in 1737 is now worth $43.

Imagine you're walking down the street with your spouse one day, and she says, "Honey, look! A *free* wine and cheese tasting!" And in you both go. Forty-three dollars later, you're back outside.

"The free wine and cheese was nice, but what a deal on this vintage bottle of wine!" Never mind that neither of you are connoisseurs of wine.

Once you went inside you felt you should buy something, not just be another freeloader off the street—even though that *was*, after all, your original plan. Of course, you were a little short of cash, so on the credit card it went.

From Franklin's perspective, you wasted $43 on something you didn't need, and you're *$86* behind those who walked right by that "free" wine tasting. How?

Well, they not only avoided owing $43, but by resisting temptation, they also had that much more to save. Forty-three dollars saved, $86 clear. It's a counterintuitive way to think about money, but you have to admit, it makes lots of cents.

Prudent spending and prudent saving are two sides of the same coin. In this chapter we'll expose and explore the biggest obstacle to retirement planning most of us face. Then we'll consider how "practicing" for retirement helps us develop smart spending—and saving—habits.

MARY'S STORY

If you've done your homework from chapter 2, you have a pretty clear idea of your purpose for retirement. You're probably even excited about the opportunities retirement offers.

If you also found yourself wondering where the money will come from to make your vision of retirement a reality, you're far from alone. A 2016 survey by the Employee Benefits Research Institute showed that less than half of us (48 percent) have taken the time to figure out if we'll have enough money for a comfortable retirement.[4]

The same poll from 2015 showed 24 percent of us lack confidence that we'll have enough to retire comfortably. That sense is mostly instinctive, but it is well founded. There is a very real obstacle almost all of us need to address in making our retirement dreams a reality. It's called the income gap.

We'll define the income gap shortly, but first I'd like you to meet Mary. She used to worry about affording retirement too—but she isn't worried any more.

Mary wanted to retire at sixty-three, after being a nurse for nearly forty years. She had a small pension but would have no medical benefits post-retirement; she'd have to go out and buy them on her own.

Because Mary earned $80,000 a year and her home was paid off, she did not have to worry about budgeting from month to month. There was always enough money in her bank accounts to meet her expenses. But when I asked Mary how much she would

---

4 Ruth Helman, Craig Copeland, and Jack VanDerhei, "The 2016 Retirement Confidence Survey: Worker Confidence Stable, Retiree Confidence Continues to Increase," *Employee Benefit Research Institute Issue Brief* no. 422 (March 2016).

need to support her lifestyle on a monthly basis, she answered with a question of her own: "Maybe $4,000 or $5,000?"

Mary was obviously taking a guess. An educated one, perhaps— but still a guess. I suggested we develop some concrete numbers for a few reasons.

First, Mary was sure to feel more confident in retirement if she understood her basic expenses. With that knowledge in place, we could determine a range of discretionary income—for things like travel—and reinforce her ability to so such things in retirement.

That's important. Some retirees become scared to spend any money, for fear of not having enough. Others, meanwhile, think they can spend more freely than their assets allow. Figuring out Mary's reality was the key to boosting her confidence.

Another reason for determining the monthly cost of Mary's lifestyle was that it would be hard to determine if she had enough saved without first knowing how much she needed.

Finally, there's something I call "practicing retirement." Until Mary became honest with herself about whether her projected monthly lifestyle expense was realistic, she'd be setting herself up for an uncertain outcome. Knowing the reality, however, would allow her to begin living within her retirement budget before she retired, to groom the spending habits that would help her realize the retirement she wanted.

We began by detailing the income Mary's pension would provide. Next, we discussed the advantages of waiting to claim Social Security and then looked at how much she would have to withdraw from her retirement accounts.

Mary had $750,000 of retirement assets, plus $10,000 of pension income each year; it was clear she'd need to make up a sizable portion of income.

Next we factored in medical insurance premiums of $6,000 until she reached Medicare age at sixty-five. Mary realized that retiring at sixty-three would put significant pressure on her hard-earned retirement assets, creating a $50,000 income gap.

On the other hand, working until sixty-five would allow Mary to save more. Her 401(k) would continue to build, helping decrease the risk of running out of money should she live an extended life expectancy.

Mary and I considered the risks of retiring at sixty-three by accurately projecting how her income flow would look. She saw the prudence in working until sixty-five, and we even discussed whether *that* was her ideal scenario—or whether working until she reached her full Social Security retirement age of sixty-six made more sense.

Just as it was for Mary, the income gap is the "elephant in the room" for almost everyone when it comes to retirement planning. It's something we all suspect is there but hesitate to talk about, due mostly to fear. Rather than meet that fear head-on like Mary did, many families procrastinate because they're convinced that taking action won't make any difference.

The thing is, it *does* make a difference! It's not only possible but essential to figure out and deal with your unique income gap, and the sooner the better. By taking action, you take the crucial first step toward securing the full, rewarding retirement you've pictured, instead of one that doesn't live up to your vision.

SO WHAT *IS* THE INCOME GAP?

When you retire, you draw the funds you'll need for living expenses—your retirement income—from fixed sources: pensions, part-time employment, Social Security, guaranteed annuities. (We'll cover the sources of retirement income fully in chapter 5.)

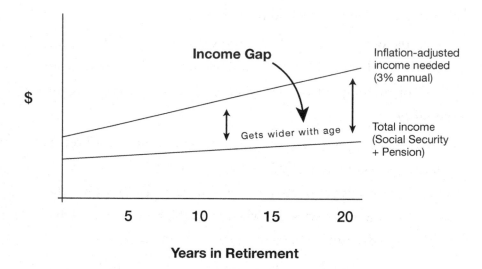

Years in Retirement

If these income sources don't cover your expenses—plus inflation, taxes, medical care, and a variety of unknown liabilities—then you end up with a "gap" between the money you have and the money you're going to need, as you get further into retirement.

That, in a nutshell, is the income gap.

Many studies have shown that almost everyone will experience an income gap at some point. How you fill it is one of the most important decisions you'll make along the way, and you can't decide how to do that with random numbers. You need to be using real numbers: your numbers.

WHICH BRINGS US TO BUDGETING

Ugh! I know. It's maybe one of the most painful things we can do. I've heard that some people actually *enjoy* budgeting—then again, it's always been an accountant who's telling me so.

Whether you love it or hate it, budgeting is the foundation of financial planning. You simply can't put together a solid retirement plan without a detailed budget; in fact, you need not one budget, but two: one for today and one for your retirement.

Remember Dr. David McClelland? He's the Harvard professor, mentioned in chapter 1, who found that the key difference between successful and less-than-successful entrepreneurs is having a plan and sticking to it.

If you think about your finances in the same way a business views profits, you want your career to have been profitable enough that you can fund your retirement goals. That means there are two basic financial statements you should focus on: balance sheets and income statements.

A balance sheet lists your current assets and liabilities.

Income statements (also called "profit and loss" statements or "cash flow" statements in the business world) are a little different. They show that you have *x* amount of money coming in and *y* amount of money going out. They tell you whether you're in the black or in the red. That's pretty much what a budget is all about, right?

Like any business's numbers, your personal finances change over time. Successful businesses do forecasting and planning to adjust for both good and bad market conditions. Doesn't it make sense to adopt the same practices for your own financial well-being?

I mentioned that you really need two budgets, one for today and one for retirement. We're going to start with the easy one, the "now" budget. In the next chapter, we'll turn to projecting expenses in retirement. The combined information you'll garner will provide your full financial picture, which is the key to identifying and bridging your retirement income gap.

That's because putting together and following a detailed "now" budget will prepare you to "practice" for retirement, when careful stewardship of your newly fixed income will be critical in making the retirement you envision a reality. Practicing adherence to a budget now will help ensure that the transition to retirement is as smooth as possible.

We'll draw up your retirement budget a bit later. For now, let's focus on fully understanding your current income and expenses.

PUTTING TOGETHER YOUR "NOW" BUDGET

The goal of your "now" budget is to get as clear and complete an idea of all your current expenses as possible and of how you allocate your income to meet them.

You're going to have some fixed costs and some that vary, just as any business does. For now—while you're still working—your biggest expense by far is the roof over your head. If your house is not paid off or you're paying rent, make that the first item of your personal budget. (And even if your home is paid off, remember, you may still have real estate taxes to pay.)

Another big necessity, of course, is food. What do you spend per week (or month, or however you want to capture it for your budget) on groceries? I recommend tracking your supermarket spending for a full month to get a solid number.

Don't forget the shirt on your back. Clothing is a necessity many people overlook when doing a personal budget because it's so easy to pull out a credit card. Paying it off, however, is the trick, especially if you haven't set the money aside to do so.

After these basic necessities—housing, food, and clothing—comes utilities: electric, cable TV, Internet, water, trash collection, all the services that provide the "creature comforts" of life.

Car payments, vehicle maintenance, and other transportation costs are another major category.

What about insuring these assets, along with yourself and your family? Homeowners insurance, car insurance, life insurance, and health coverage, right?

Together, these comprise what I call the "big six" categories of living expenses:

1. Housing
2. Food
3. Clothing
4. Utilities
5. Transportation
6. Insurance

We're still not done. There are miscellaneous expenses—like lawn care—and "unexpected" ones we really should expect: things like car repairs and replacing a hot water heater or a roof. To budget for such seasonal and maintenance-related expenses, it's wise to set funds aside on a regular basis and let them build. It sure beats pulling out a credit card.

Don't forget out-of-pocket medical costs. Assuming you're relatively healthy and have health insurance through your employer, use last year's total as a guide. Include things like co-pays, diagnostic tests that your plan may not cover, and fees for dental and eye care.

Medical expenses, especially for retirees, constitute a huge expense. We'll address their impact during retirement in the next chapter, but be warned—an extended illness at any age can quickly drain your assets. In this area perhaps more than any other, erring on the side of caution by setting aside extra funds can help protect your retirement savings makes tremendous sense.

The final area to factor into your budget is variable and discretionary expenditures: club memberships, dining out, entertainment (movies, sporting events, theater, museums, etc.), personal travel expenses (like vacations and family visits), donations to charities, and gifts to friends and relatives. This category is likely to increase when you retire and have exponentially more time on your hands, especially early in retirement, when you are healthy.

Budgeting is all about anticipation. You know you'll have certain expenses, but many are easy to overlook. Whatever you do, don't try to capture them all from memory. Sit down with your checking account records from the last year and add up your expenditures in each category. And don't forget those maintenance items! You know they're coming too. Saving for them now could save you long-term debt later.

Credit card statements are another good source of information about purchases you're making; don't overlook automatic payments that might be charged to a card or those that might be drawn from your savings account instead of your checking account.

Once you've identified all your expenses—ongoing and potential—put together a full breakdown of where and when your money is going.

Finally and perhaps most important, don't downplay or "lowball" your expenses. Instead, be conservative. Figure you'll spend a bit *more* than you have in the past because, after all, when was the last time the cost of anything went *down*?

The knowledge you'll gain from assembling and tracking all your expenses in one place will help you spend more wisely. That's going to be very important as you close in on retirement.

There's another plus. By writing out a budget and then comparing it to reality once or twice a month when you pay your bills, you may begin to silence that uncertain little voice that keeps saying, "You'll never afford retirement." Following a budget builds confidence and uncovers places where you're overspending or buying things you really don't need—money that instead could be put toward filling your retirement income gap.

People procrastinate planning for retirement because they fear being unable to afford it, but without a budget, they really don't know. With one, they quickly realize that being deliberate about saving a "penny" is the key to becoming "two pence clear."

●——— HOMEWORK: PREPARE YOUR PERSONAL BUDGET ———●

Nearly all of us will have to overcome an income gap in retirement. Creating a "now" budget is the first step in doing so. In chapter 4, you'll take the second step: identifying your expenses during retirement and learning how things like medical expenses, inflation, and personal debt contribute to your income gap.

Your homework for this chapter is to get a detailed understanding of your current expenditures and how you meet them. This will lead to spending more wisely, allowing you to set more money aside for your future.

Will you miraculously discover a spare million dollars? Of course not. But even if it's $40 a week, that's over $2,000 a year. Along with your 401(k) at work, tax strategies, and other approaches we'll cover later, that can become a foundational part of your total retirement plan.

Sharpen your pencil enough, and you might find $60, $80, or $100 per week—or more. But you won't know—you *can't* know—without putting together a thorough, detailed personal spending plan.

Using the descriptions in the last section and the worksheet on the opposite page, identify every expenditure you make to create a budget that is easy to update as your expenses change. Treating your personal finances like a business will serve you well for the rest of your life and never better than in retirement—the potential expenses of which we'll cover in detail in chapter 4.

CURRENT BUDGET

Home Expenses		Transportation	
Mortage		Vehicle Payments	
Real Estate Taxes		Fuel	
Electricity		Tolls	
Gas/Oil		Repairs	
Water/Sewer/Trash		Registration/License	
Cell Phone		Other	
Cable/Satellite		Insurance	
Internet		Auto	
Furnishings/Appliances		Health	
Lawn/Garden		Home/Rental	
Home Supplies		Life Insurance	
Maintenance		Personal Umbrella	
Improvements		Health	
Other		Doctor/Dentist	
Daily Living		Medicine/Rx	
Groceries		Health Club Dues	
Personal Supplies		Other	
Clothing		Professional Services	
Cleaning Services		Accounting	
Dining/Eating Out		Legal	
Travel		Financial Advisory	
Dry Cleaning		Charity/Gifts	
Salon/Personal Care		Tax Deductible Gifts	
Discretionary		Personal Gifts	
Children		Miscellaneous	
School Tuition		Vacation	
School Lunch		Hobbies	
School Supplies		Other	
Babysitting/Daycare			
Activities			
Debt/Liabilities			
Credit Card			
Personal Debt			
Other		Total	

CHAPTER 4

BUDGETING FOR RETIREMENT

"An investment in knowledge pays the best interest."

As we've already seen, retirement without a purpose can quickly become a long slog through uneventful days instead of a vibrant, joyous capstone to a life well lived.

The work you've already done to identify your passions and define your ideal retirement will help chart your course. Your homework from chapter 3 provided a much clearer picture of your current expenses, and probably got you thinking about the costs of the retirement you want to live.

Helping you realize that vision is what the rest of this book is all about.

Think of it as an investment in knowledge, exactly the kind Ben Franklin was referring to in his quote. The interest you'll earn? Confidence. The knowledge that, with careful planning and the help of a trusted financial advisor, you're much more likely to bridge your income gap and enjoy the retirement you envision.

THE INCOME GAP, PART TWO

In studying the income gap thus far, we've met Mary, a nursing professional who worried, like so many of us do, about affording retirement. Instead of letting that fear paralyze her, Mary acted—and through her work with me, discovered that the key to a workable financial plan for retirement is considering many possible scenarios.

We've talked about how the Federal Reserve "stress-tests" its policy decisions to see which are the wisest, based on a host of factors. Similarly, we must consider all the factors impacting our personal finances in retirement. How do they increase—or help to bridge— your income gap? This really captures the process I follow in building financial plans to take clients through retirement.

The personal budget you just completed has provided you with a deeper understanding of your income and expenses than you've ever had. That will serve you well indeed as we shift our focus to factors that might impact your assets as retirement approaches. Let's start with a close look at the potential effects of inflation.

MEET JIM

Like many clients, Jim first contacted me when he was sixty years old, having realized retirement planning could no longer wait.

Jim was married and in good health. Current research shows that when both partners live to age sixty-five, there's a nearly 50 percent chance at least one will also see their ninetieth birthday. Jim's wife Carol was in good health too, so we agreed it was wise to plan for a twenty-five-year retirement. Based on information Jim provided about their lifestyle, housing situation, and the retirement they pictured for themselves, we projected Jim and Carol's expenses during retirement to be $5,000 a month, an annual total of $60,000.

Sounds pretty straightforward, right? But additional factors can change this "raw" number over the course of retirement, and one is inflation.

We hear about the "inflation rate" in economic reports, but what is it, exactly?

Inflation measures the combined effect of changes to the prices of everyday goods and services *and* in the purchasing power of money. For Jim and Carol, we chose an inflation factor of 3 percent per year—a bit higher than the long-term trend of 2.26 percent—so we'd be safe.

Factored for each of the five years until Jim would retire at age sixty-five, that 3 percent inflation rate had a profound impact. It increased the couple's total expenses in their first year of retirement to $69,556, almost $10,000 more than our initial figure.

If that seems surprising, hold onto your hat.

After ten years, inflation grew Jim and Carol's annual expenses to $80,000. (That's just five years into retirement because—remember—our calculations began the year Jim first sat down with me, five years before retirement.)

By age ninety, based on that conservative 3 percent inflation estimate alone, they'd need $125,000 per year. Adding up our inflation-adjusted projections across their twenty-five-year retirement produced a total $2,612,039.

That $2.6 million sounds scary, right? But it's also very static.

For one thing, if Jim or Carol dies before age ninety, there'll be a decrease in living expenses for the survivor. We can't know when or if that will happen, however, so we're smarter to plan based on both reaching ninety.

Another consideration: for the twelve months before I started writing this book, the US inflation rate was just 1.1 percent, well below the longer-term average of 2.26 percent. So why use 3 percent? Are we being too conservative?

INFLATION AND RETIREMENT

I don't think so, and here's why.

The Consumer Price Index (CPI) was created to measure monthly changes in the prices of consumer goods and services. It uses two hundred categories to get a factor—an "index"—of how prices are behaving.

CPI is a real benchmark metric, one essential for calculating inflation. As we'll see in the next section, the Social Security Administration uses CPI to figure the annual cost of living adjustments it provides to recipients.

While inflation has averaged just over 1 percent in the recent short term, it's averaged 2.26 percent across the past twenty years, and closer to 2.5 percent if you go back even further.[5] On top of this, a retiree's living expenses are going to be much different than someone who is younger, has a family, and is working.

In fact, the differences for retirees are significant enough that there's a whole *separate* CPI for older folks, the CPI-E (the "E" is for "elderly").

---

5 "Consumer Price Index," US Department of Labor—Bureau of Labor Statistics, http://www.bls.gov/cpi/.

CPI-E tracks prices for people over sixty-two and older. It has consistently hovered around 3.1 percent, and none of us should be surprised by perhaps the biggest reason: medical expenses.

That higher inflation rate for elders is why I hedge my calculations and round my inflation factor up to 3 percent for retirees. Doing so more than covers the overall inflation rate at its historical high, with over half a percent to spare—and when planning for retirement (or anything else), it's always best to err on the side of caution. I also suggest to clients that as they consider their individual expenses, they should use different inflation rates based on the individual expenses. For example, core living expenses most likely track close to traditional CPI. However, medical expenses are accelerating at a much higher rate. Travel is another expense that typically increases faster than CPI.

COST OF LIVING AND SOCIAL SECURITY

We can't fully consider the effect of retirement income and expenses on your income gap without discussing that old stalwart of the American retirement landscape, Social Security. We'll cover Social Security's overall impact on retirement income later, but before we move on from inflation, it's helpful to understand how it might impact your Social Security benefits.

Each year, the Social Security Administration calculates a cost-of-living adjustment (COLA) to the payments it makes to recipients. While "inflation" and "cost of living" are used interchangeably in the media, there's a fine difference. As we've just seen, the inflation rate is derived from the combination of the cost of goods (CPI) and the purchasing power of money. The COLAs that Social Security makes, however, are based on CPI alone—and lately, I've noticed some concerning changes in their enactment.

COLAs, for want of a better term, are essentially a "raise" for Social Security recipients; an incremental annual increase designed to help benefits keep up with the prices of essential goods and services.

From 2009 going all the way back to 1975, when COLAs were first instituted, Social Security recipients got their raise; the program increased payments in every one of those thirty-five years. More recently, however—in three of the seven years from 2010 through 2016—guess what? No raise.

According to a study by the Senior Citizens League in 2016, the cost of living for people over age sixty-five increased 74 percent between 2000 and 2015. Yet during that same period, COLAs from Social Security totaled just 43 percent. **That's a 31 percent shortfall.**[6] Take a look.

SENIOR'S COST OF LIVING 2000–15: SELECTED PRICE CHANGES

Expense	Percent Change
Apartment rental	56%
Property tax	127%
Gasoline	76%
Medical (out of pocket)	30%
Dental	83%
Medical Part D*	50%
Medigap	100%
Movie ticket	52%
Milk (gallon)	35%
Ground chuck	130%
Chicken	46%

6 "2015 Senior Survey Results," The Senior Citizens League, May 22, 2015, http://seniorsleague. org/2015-senior-survey-results/.

Clearly, Social Security is failing to keep up with increases to the cost of living. As we saw in the last section, we must compensate for that.

Beyond Social Security's COLAs, what you pay for essential goods and services might also be affected by *where* you retire. If you plan on living in a different region or country, the expenses particular to that locale must also be taken into account.

LIVING EXPENSES AND LONG-TERM DEBT

Wherever you retire, the *types* of expenses you will face remain constant. We identified the "big six" necessities of life in chapter 3:

1. Housing

2. Food

3. Clothing

4. Utilities

5. Transportation

6. Insurance

Projecting your costs in these areas as you formulate your retirement plan—and taking steps now to keep them as low as possible—will prove crucial in holding your income gap to a minimum.

Consider each category carefully, and don't forget seasonal, maintenance, and miscellaneous expenses.

It is critically important as you approach retirement to get a good handle on your long-term debt. Whether it's a mortgage, credit cards, or something else, being locked into long-term payments puts real pressure on your monthly cash flow, especially retirement, when you're living on a fixed income. And needless to say, the bigger the payment, the greater the impact.

A mortgage is usually the largest monthly obligation we face. I recommend exploring every realistic option for paying off your home by the time you retire. But don't forget, even paid-off houses come with continuing costs: taxes, maintenance, homeowners insurance, plus the cost of utilities. And the larger your home, the higher these costs will be.

If paying off your mortgage isn't possible or cost effective, consider changing your housing situation. Selling your large home and downsizing to one bought with the equity makes sense for many people, especially if it eliminates mortgage payments.

You might also invest the equity from your sold house and rent, using gains on your investments to help shoulder your rental costs. You'll still have a monthly payment, but maintenance expenses will shift to your landlord.

Options do exist, but there may be fewer than you realize. Ranch-style, single-level living, particularly in areas not traditionally thought of as retirement meccas—like Minnesota—can be hard to find. Homes and even apartments with ground-level access are in great demand. Even though you're downsizing, you might pay the same or even more each month than you are now.

Clearly then, the living arrangement you choose for retirement depends on what is most cost effective for your situation. Just remember that "cost effective" means a home in which you can be comfortable, preferably with a small monthly payment—or better yet, none at all.

I strongly discourage retirees from using a home equity loan or "reverse mortgage," as they're often marketed these days. That's just robbing Peter to pay Paul, borrowing from yourself to pay yourself, while the bank collects some money in between. It's typically better to liquidate, to sell and use the equity for retirement income. (We'll look more closely at reverse mortgages later in the book.)

Personal loans, auto loans, credit cards—we all use these sources of long-term debt at various points in our lives, but you really should make it a priority to mitigate and, to whatever extent you can, eliminate them as you head into retirement. Long-term debt is extremely toxic in regard to preserving your sources of retirement income.

LONGEVITY AND YOUR LEGACY

We've mentioned it already, but it bears repeating: we're living longer than ever. That means we must preserve our retirement savings as long as possible. By holding substantial balances in investment mechanisms as long as possible, you give your money its best opportunity for growth. That's crucial, if your retirement income is going to last as long as you do.

The amount you need isn't a static number; if it were, you could just retire in your fifties, withdraw a percentage each year, and be in great shape. That's just not realistic. Hypothetically, your withdrawal rate should accelerate as you get older, when you need it most.

It would be so much easier if we only knew how long we're going to live! We can't, of course, but we can plan conservatively, as I did with Jim and Carol. It's best to plan on living longer than you think. If things don't turn out that way, you can pass whatever's left to family, friends, or a favorite charity.

Indeed, that's the final consideration on the expense side of your retirement budget. Do you want to leave a legacy behind? If so, you'll want to factor it into your retirement expenses. If leaving a legacy is not as important, that might allow a slightly more aggressive withdrawal rate from your retirement accounts.

●——— HOMEWORK: YOUR EXPENSES IN RETIREMENT ———●

In this chapter we've looked closely at factors that can affect your expenses in retirement and learned, in a big-picture way, how they might affect your income gap. We've seen the importance of eliminating long-term debt, but even then, inflation can and very likely will cause your living expenses to escalate during your retirement years.

To get an idea of how much, you must first project the expenses you'll face in your first year of retirement. Begin with the "now" budget you completed in chapter 3, and adjust it to reflect the expenses you anticipate when you're ready to retire, based on whether your home will be paid off, the existence of other long-term debt, and where you plan to live.

Once you have what you feel is a solid number for that first year, use the following chart to quickly gauge the effects of differing inflation rates over various numbers of years in retirement.

Number of years	Inflation Rates			
	2%	3%	4%	5%
5	1.104	1.159	1.217	1.276
10	1.219	1.344	1.480	1.629
15	1.346	1.558	1.801	2.079
20	1.486	1.806	2.191	2.653
25	1.641	2.094	2.666	3.386
30	1.811	2.427	3.243	4.322

This exercise will help you to understand how inflation, coupled with major expenses, can quickly expand your income gap. In part two, we'll turn to bridging your income gap, as we explore in detail all your options for saving and wisely investing, with the goal of building lifelong retirement income.

PART ONE SUMMARY

Part one and its homework laid the foundation for the rest of this book. Here's what we've covered so far.

CHAPTER 1

WHY YOU NEED A FINANCIAL PLAN FOR RETIREMENT

- ◎ We're living longer than ever before, and more of us are retiring early—a "double-whammy" that means we must plan more carefully for retirement than our parents and grandparents did.

- ◎ There's no magic formula for a happy retirement. Just as your doctor diagnoses your physical condition, prescribes appropriate treatment, and follows up regularly, so your retirement plan must be based on your current financial condition and your future needs and desires.

- ◎ It is crucial to stress-test your retirement plan against various economic conditions sure to impact it.

CHAPTER 2

YOUR FUTURE: RETIREMENT GOALS AND DESIRES

- ◎ We met Gary, who retired early without a solid idea of what he'd do with his free time. Gary's story showed the importance of having a purpose in retirement.

- ◎ In just one generation, the responsibility for a successful retirement has shifted almost entirely—from our employers, to us.

- ◎ Homework: Take the first step in formulating your retirement plan by clearly defining the retirement you want to live.

CHAPTER 3

THE ELEPHANT IN THE ROOM: YOUR INCOME GAP

- ◎ People delay planning for retirement because they fear the income gap, the difference between the expenses they'll still face in retirement and the fixed income available to them.

- ◎ The income gap is real, but a brave woman named Mary showed how procrastination is not the answer. Defining it and developing a plan now provides your best chance for bridging it.

◎ How you spend money today affects how you'll retire tomorrow. Practice for retirement by cultivating wise spending habits now, while you're still working.

◎ Homework: Develop a personal budget, the best tool for cultivating those wise fiscal habits.

CHAPTER 4

BUDGETING FOR RETIREMENT

◎ There are important steps you can take to reduce and offset your income gap.

◎ Jim and Carol's story showed the potential—and very profound—effects of inflation.

◎ Where you choose to retire impacts on your cost of living. So do your "big six" expenses.

◎ Homework: Project your living expenses in retirement, and see how inflation will affect them.

In part two, we explore tools and strategies that can help secure the retirement you envision.

PART TWO

CREATING, PROTECTING, AND DRAWING RETIREMENT INCOME

CHAPTER 5

RETIREMENT SAVINGS OPTIONS AND HOW THEY WORK

"Life is difficult. This is a great truth, one of the greatest truths. It is a great truth because once we truly see this truth, we transcend it."

—M. SCOTT PECK, *THE ROAD LESS TRAVELED*

If you took nothing else from part one, I hope you learned this: the responsibility for saving the money needed to take you through retirement has shifted. In prior generations, most workers could count on employer-funded plans for the bulk of their retirement income.

Today, funding your retirement is primarily on you.

Is that a good thing? I guess it depends on whether you're a glass-half-empty or glass-half-full sort of person, though I doubt any retiree who benefited from one would call the employer-funded, guaranteed pensions our parents and grandparents relied on "bad."

Still, the truth is inescapable. Such plans are disappearing fast. We need to accept that truth and learn about tools and strategies for dealing with it. That's what part two is all about.

We actually have plenty of options for establishing retirement savings, and we'll cover them in this chapter. Growing those savings through wise investing can be a big key to overcoming your income gap, so we'll study investment strategies in chapter 6. In chapter 7, we'll learn how taxes can take a much bigger bite than necessary, unless you're smart about how, when, and from where you draw retirement income. Chapter 8 covers options for protecting your retirement savings and other assets, and chapter 9 looks at establishing an estate plan for passing your legacy along.

Let's begin with your tools for building retirement savings.

EMPLOYER-SPONSORED RETIREMENT SAVINGS PLANS

For generations, employer-sponsored plans have been the backbone of retirement savings and income for Americans. They still are, but most are a far cry from the employer-funded pensions our parents enjoyed.

401(K)-TYPE PLANS

Today, most employers instead offer what's called a *traditional* 401(k).

If you work for a nonprofit or the government, you might have a *403(b)* or *457* plan. The 403(b) is typically offered by educational and certain nonprofit organizations, while 457s are the retirement saving tool typically offered by government agencies.

But wait, there's more! Small employers might offer SEP and SIMPLE IRAs. Similar to the "400 series" plans just listed, these are specially designed to give employees and owners of small companies equivalent opportunities to save significant money for retirement.

Together these comprise a category called *defined contribution plans*, and each works the same way. Employees—the plan's documents usually call them "participants"—*define* the amount they'll contribute, and each participant has their own account. (For our purposes here, I refer to all plans of this category as "401(k)-type plans.")

Most participants fund their accounts with pre-tax earnings. Some employers offer the option of contributing from after-tax (net) pay (more on those "Roth-type" plans in a moment).

Besides the contributions employees make from their paychecks, some employers offer to "match" them, usually up to a given percentage of the employee's total salary. Those percentages vary from employer to employer. Some might make contributions as a form of profit sharing, whether in addition to or in place of the percentage match.

The maximum employee contribution is subject to change, but as I write this book in 2016, participants below the age of fifty can set aside up to $18,000 per year. If you're fifty or older, you can make "catch-up" deposits of an additional $6,000, for a maximum of $24,000 per year.

If your employer offers a match and/or profit sharing, the *combination* of their contributions and yours cannot exceed $53,000 per year, whatever your age. High-income earners who get a large employer match and/or profit sharing take note, because this limit could come into play. (Again, these are the limits as I write. Consult a financial advisor for the current numbers.)

Most 401(k) participants choose the traditional, tax-deferred option. Contributions come out of their gross pay, and taxes are deferred on both the principal and on any appreciation—the gains made through investments—until they start taking distributions in retirement.

This option has two big advantages. Besides delaying the tax liability on your retirement savings, contributing to the plan from your gross pay lowers your taxable income. That means you pay less income tax while you're still in the workforce. Depending on your situation, however, it might actually benefit you to consider the after-tax option, if your employer offers it.

This is known as a "Roth 401(k)." Your contribution is taken from your net pay instead of your gross. The advantage? You never pay taxes on your money again—neither the principal nor any appreciation. But depending on your bigger picture, the Roth option may not be your best choice, either.

We'll look harder at both tax-deferred and Roth-type plans in the next two chapters, when we consider investment strategies and the tax ramifications of drawing on your retirement savings.

PENSIONS

As already discussed, employer-funded pensions—defined benefit plans—are quickly vanishing, but they still factor prominently in the retirement resources of many baby boomers. If you're one of them, you should feel truly blessed and fortunate.

Once the gold standard of retirement, pensions used to be widely offered by both public- and private-sector employers. Together with Social Security benefits, they pretty much guaranteed seniors a financially secure retirement. These days, however, few private-sector employers offer pension plans, due to their cost and the profit demands of stockholders.

Most of the pensions still being offered today, therefore, go to state and federal government workers and employees of public education institutions like school districts and state colleges. The longer the employee stays, the bigger their defined benefit. This guarantee of income in retirement helps public-service entities retain workers, many of whom could be making much higher salaries in the private sector.

Pensions are a cornerstone of public service compensation. The advantages are numerous:

◎ The employer makes all contributions (in most cases).

◎ The employees are not responsible for choosing investments, thereby eliminating the risk of making bad investment decisions.

◎ Employees typically know how much they will receive, based on earnings and length of service at retirement.

◎ The employee pays no tax until they begin drawing money in retirement.

I'd include a similar list of the disadvantages of pensions, but it's just not that long! For workers, pensions are the goose that lays the golden egg. There are, however, a couple of very important—if rare—risks.

First, the performance of the investments your employer chooses to back your pension could affect its solvency. If things go wrong, then there's a small chance you wouldn't get the full benefit, even though pensions are federally insured.

Perhaps more worrisome is that public-sector pensions have come under increasing attack, particularly in states experiencing budget crises. Just a few years ago in Wisconsin, lawmakers cut the state's pension contributions in half and required employees to contribute the difference. If you work in a cash-strapped state, it's smart to keep on top of developments in your legislature—and, if possible, have alternate sources of retirement savings.

OTHER TYPES OF RETIREMENT SAVINGS PLANS

Though employer-sponsored plans like 401(k)s and pensions are the most common, there are a host of other tools for building retirement savings. IRAs, Social Security, and investment portfolios top the list.

IRAs—individual retirement arrangements—offer tax advantages like employer-sponsored plans do but are opened and directed entirely by you. They also offer unlimited investment choices for growing the principal you put in: stocks, bonds, mutual funds, annuities, CDs, money market funds, real estate—all of these investments can be held in an IRA.

Let me be clear: the IRA *itself* is not the investment. It's an account, just like a 401(k)-type plan, a place you put money to save for retirement. It's the investment choices you make for the money within the account that drive your savings' growth.

You've probably heard of traditional and Roth IRAs. There's also what's called a "Roth conversion IRA," 401(k)-to-IRA rollovers, and others. These options might help you save more efficiently and reduce your tax liability in retirement. We'll detail them in the next two chapters. For now, let's focus on the two most common types of IRA: traditional and Roth.

TRADITIONAL IRAS

Like the money employees put in traditional 401(k)-type plans at work, contributions to a traditional IRA can be deducted on your income tax. Limits are based on your income and set by the IRS.

Besides the reduction in current income (and therefore, income tax) thanks to your contributions, you pay no taxes on those contributions, or on gains from investing them, until you start taking money out of your IRA in retirement.

Contribution limits differ depending which side of age fifty you are on. Folks fifty and older can put away additional funds per year, a "catch-up" provision for increasing savings as retirement gets closer.

Probably the biggest plus with a traditional IRA is that you can make a contribution until the tax deadline of April 15, and deduct it on the return you're about to file—the one documenting your income in the prior year. This means you can make a contribution in April to reduce last year's tax bill just as it comes due.

Whether a traditional IRA is right for you depends on your other retirement savings, your income, and your filing status. Here's a quick example, showing the basics of contributing to a traditional IRA.

Spouses John and Jane are under fifty years of age. John works and has a 401(k) with his employer. Jane is a stay-at-home mom. She takes care of the kids and runs the household but has no earned income. John and Jane file their taxes jointly.

John makes below the income limit for contributing to a traditional IRA. Though Jane does not have earned income, she qualifies for an account of her own. That means John and Jane can set up separate IRAs, contribute the maximum to both, and fully deduct the contributions on their joint tax return. At the IRS-established limits in effect as I write, each could each contribute $5,500, for a total deduction of $11,000 against their income.

One important note: While many focus on getting that tax deduction, you're allowed to contribute to an IRA regardless of whether you meet the deduction rules. Contributing right up to the limit is perfectly legal, even if you can't claim the deduction. Doing so actually makes sense in some cases, but in many others, contributing to a Roth IRA instead is the better choice.

HELP WITH MEDICAL EXPENSES: HSAs AND FSAs

The harder you find it to save for retirement, the more susceptible your savings become to a simple fact of life: As we age, our health declines. Medical expenses can quickly decimate even significant savings, but three savings tools modeled on IRAs might help.

Health savings accounts (HSAs) and *flexible savings accounts* (FSAs) are designed to help you meet out-of-pocket medical expenses. Both are funded with pre-tax contributions from you and—in some cases—your employer, and you never pay tax on withdrawals that cover qualified medical expenses.

HSAs are available only to people with HDHPs: *high-deductible health insurance plans,* as defined by the IRS. People without HDHPs can open FSAs to save for future medical expenses.

Another type of plan, *limited-purpose FSAs*, are used to supplement HSAs, covering dental and vision care.

All three plans follow strict rules, which include penalties for nonqualified withdrawals. Features within employer-administered versions vary from one employer to the next.

Consult a qualified financial advisor to learn how one or a combination of these plans can help cover the increasing—and, as you age, inevitable—cost of medical care, while preserving as much of your retirement savings as possible.

ROTH IRAS

Though the contribution limits, effects of filing status, and income guidelines are the same with Roth IRAs as for traditional ones, Roth plans carry several key differences.

First and foremost, there are no deducting contributions to a Roth IRA on your tax return. Sounds like a big sacrifice, but guess what? Like the Roth 401(k) we've already covered, *you never pay taxes* on income from your Roth IRA. Every dollar you put in, and the gains you realize through investment—for the entire life of the account—is yours. Uncle Sam doesn't get one cent.

Another big difference is that, with a traditional IRA, you must start withdrawing specific amounts each year—called *required minimum distributions* (RMDs)—beginning in the year you turn age seventy and a half. Not so with a Roth IRA. Your money can continue to grow, tax free, for as long as you'd like, and no distributions are required.

Just like traditional IRAs, Roths give you unlimited investment choices. The catch-up provision for people fifty and older applies too.

More good news: Remember John and Jane? They can have more earned income—a lot more—than they could under a traditional IRA and still contribute the maximum to Roth IRAs, one in each of their names.

Whichever type of IRA you're considering, a trusted financial advisor can give you the current income and contribution limits.

What's that? Why, you ask, would anybody even *think* about a traditional IRA, given what we just learned about the tax advantages of a Roth? I understand. At first blush, the Roth sounds like the best way to go, hands-down.

Whether it is, however, depends on many factors, things you simply might not consider on your own—for example, your current tax rate, versus the rate you anticipate in retirement. Balance is the key, and ensuring you achieve the proper balance for your particular situation is where your financial advisor can really earn his keep.

There are products that sound like "sure things" all across the financial product landscape, but remember, there is no such thing as a sure thing, and the more carefully you plan, the more likely you are to select the right balance of retirement savings vehicles—and ultimately, to realize your retirement goals.

SOCIAL SECURITY

Let's shift gears to a whole different realm of retirement savings—or really, income: Social Security. The origins of this longtime government program date to Germany in 1889, forty-six years before President Franklin D. Roosevelt duplicated it here. The Germans wanted to get aging workers out of the factories so a younger, more productive workforce could replace them.

Social Security is funded by a payroll tax on employers and their employees. Both pay the same amount. (If you're self-employed, you pay both portions.) Your benefit—the monthly amount Social Security pays you—is based on your earnings history and when you claim eligibility, which can be as early as age sixty-two.

Social Security's goal of constantly rejuvenating the workforce is somewhat ironic, given what's happened to worker demographics since the program's inception.

For starters, we're all living longer. Many believe it may be necessary to raise the retirement age if Social Security is to remain viable, something that's happened only once so far, back in 1983.

Perhaps more critical to the fiscal challenges facing Social Security is that back in 1945, one person was taking benefits for every forty-two people working. By 2011, the ratio was one beneficiary to just *two* workers.[7] For a program funded by a tax on current wages, that's a big deal; the math just doesn't add up. If Social Security is going to be there for our retirement and our children's too, something must change.

The first question most people ask me about Social Security is whether it will be there for them.

Most experts agree that, with no changes, Social Security can continue to pay 100 percent of benefits through the year 2033, after which 79 percent will be funded. Clearly, some changes will be needed for people to continue getting their full benefit. I'm hoping Congress doesn't wait until the eleventh hour, but if its track record is any indication, plans for saving Social Security probably won't get to the floor until 2032.

---

7 "Fast Facts & Figures About Social Security, 2011," Social Security Administration, https://www.ssa.gov/policy/docs/chartbooks/fast_facts/2011/fast_facts11.html#oasdi.

Once people realize that Social Security isn't going to simply disappear today or tomorrow, their questions shift: They're most interested in when to apply for benefits and how to maximize them. We'll explore strategies for maximizing all your retirement income later. For now, let's get an overview of how Social Security works and how the monthly amount you'll receive is affected by when you claim benefits.

Social Security's payment formula takes your thirty-five highest years of earnings, indexes them for inflation, derives an average, and then calculates what's called your "primary insurance amount" (PIA). Many retirees think that stands for something else—but no, PIA is the amount you'll receive at what Social Security calls "full retirement age."

Once you've claimed benefits, they are subject to annual COLAs—but cost of living adjustments. As noted in chapter 4, there have recently—for the first time since COLAs were instituted—been a few years where no COLA was made.

The biggest potential adjustment to your PIA, however, relies on whether you claim benefits before, at, or later than your designated "full retirement age." This chart shows how profound that adjustment can be.

Apply at age	If FRA = 66	If FRA = 67
62	75.0%	70%
63	80.0%	75%
64	86.7%	80%
65	93.3%	86.7%
66	100%	93.3%
67		100%

When you claim your benefits determines the percentage of your PIA.

Apply at any age	Benefit will be % of PIA if FRA=66	Benefit will be % of PIA if FRA=67
66	100%	93.3%
67	108%	100%
68	116%	108%
69	124%	116%
70	132%	124%

And if you delay past full retirement age, you get an 8 percent annual credit.

It's important to note that Social Security's "full retirement age" is being adjusted, thanks to the longer life expectancies we've already discussed. If you were born between 1943 and 1954, that age is sixty-six. If you're in that group and you claim Social Security at sixty-two, as the chart shows, then your benefit will be 25 percent below your PIA. If your full retirement age is sixty-seven and you claim at age sixty-two, then your payment will be 30 percent less.

Similarly, if you wait until you must take benefits at age seventy, your benefit increases by 8 percent per year. That's simple interest, not compounded. So, if your full retirement age is sixty-six and you don't claim benefits until you turn seventy, you would net a 32 percent increase.

Though everybody would like to wait, for some it's just not realistic. It can put too much pressure on other assets (like investments or a pension) or significantly impact your lifestyle. You might need to claim Social Security earlier.

So the answer to "When should I claim Social Security benefits?" depends greatly on determining the best sequence for drawing on your retirement assets to bridge your income gap. We'll cover Social Security in greater detail in chapter 7.

YOUR INVESTMENT PORTFOLIO

Besides the investments you choose for your IRA and 401(k)-type plans, you might hold nonqualified accounts, so called because they're not tax advantaged specifically for retirement. Also called brokerage accounts, these host your stock market portfolio of non-retirement-plan investments. They can be an important financial resource that complements your retirement savings and offers instant liquidity for major expenditures in the here-and-now.

The investments held in your nonqualified account might include stocks, bonds, mutual funds, CDs at the bank, and different types of annuities (insurance vehicles designed to produce income). We'll look at each of these in the next chapter; for now, keep in mind that this option exists, beyond your holdings in the self-directed and employer-sponsored plans geared specifically to retirement, which we've already outlined.

ANNUITIES

Whether you're a baby boomer on the cusp of retiring or a forward-thinking member of the Gen-X or millennial generations, you've likely heard of annuities. It's likely that what you've heard about these vehicles has you a bit confused.

The insurance industry, which created and thereby cornered the annuities market, has saturated the media with advertising about these instruments. Unfortunately, the ads offer precious little information to help people determine whether annuities might be beneficial to their financial plans, so people call the number on their screen in hopes of figuring things out. Sometimes, however, aggressive sales reps will turn curious interest in these vehicles into done deals—

leaving many boomers who have purchased annuities without a full understanding of how they actually work.

Annuities *can* help *some* people manage their income streams during retirement. They're a longevity tool that can help protect your money. If you expect to live to a ripe old age, an annuity might help fill your income gap by synchronizing how you draw on a portion of your retirement savings.

Still—despite what some of the people *selling* them have to say— not everyone needs an annuity, and they are *not* growth vehicles. You simply cannot grow retirement savings as profoundly or efficiently with annuities as you can through wisely investing the funds you've saved in some of the vehicles we've already discussed.

We'll learn more about when annuities do and don't make sense in chapter 7.

OTHER POTENTIAL RETIREMENT INCOME

There are a few other sources of retirement income to consider.

Employment income and retirement may seem mutually exclusive, but today more people age sixty-five and up are still working, whether full- or part-time, than at any point since January 1965: 18.9 percent, according to a 2016 report from *Bloomberg News*.[8] The number had dipped below 11 percent in the mid-1980s, but it has risen steadily ever since.

Why? For one thing, the income you're permitted to earn is seriously curtailed after you've claimed Social Security benefits. Since the "official" retirement age has not kept pace with our increased

---

8 Ben Steverman, "'I'll Never Retire': Americans Break Record for Working Past 65," Bloomberg, May 13, 2016, http://www.bloomberg.com/news/articles/2016-05-13/-i-ll-never-retire-americans-break-record-for-working-past-65.

longevity, people have realized that working later in life can be a great hedge against their income gaps.

Working can also help retires solve the "time gap," all those extra hours retirement requires them to fill. The chance to interact with others for a few hours a week—say, at the local hardware store, while mixing up paint—can help keep your mind sharp, get you out of the house, and put some extra money in your pocket.

What about **inheritances** or **gifts** you might receive? As someone who creates conservative financial plans for people from all walks of life, my advice is simple. Unless you know for certain how much you'll receive and when, omit these from your financial plan.

The circumstances of others' lives can change in a heartbeat and often, quite literally, do. That's why I leave "anticipated" inheritances and gifts out of the equation. If you're fortunate enough to receive these extra dollars, then let them be a pleasant surprise because they will only help your situation.

Finally, there's what I feel is nearly always a bad retirement income option for seniors: **reverse mortgages**, which I mentioned briefly in chapter 4.

These are loans marketed heavily to retirees by celebrities from the generations that the companies are targeting. Folks like Henry Winkler ("the Fonz" on the TV show *Happy Days*), the late actor Fred Thompson, and even game show host Chuck Woolery have promoted reverse mortgages.

Issued by the Federal Housing Administration, reverse mortgages are home equity loans, taken out after your house is paid off. You must be age sixty-two or older to qualify, and there can be no liens or outstanding mortgages on the property.

Reverse mortgages provide a lump sum, a regular payment, or a combination of both. The amount is based on your home's value, your credit score, your life expectancy, and current interest rates. I view them as a *possible* alternative only when *both* of two conditions exist: (1) you just don't have enough other retirement savings, and (2) you're absolutely determined never to leave that home.

If you're willing to sell the home and move, my advice is to do so. Get the full equity, give yourself the income you need, and find a different housing arrangement. Reverse mortgages just don't make economic sense; all you're really doing is paying interest to receive some of *your own equity* in return—equity you worked to build over the course of your lifetime. Why pay interest on that money, let alone the fees you'll incur for the loan's origination?

Unless that second factor also applies—you simply can't bear to give the property up—I find these loans hard to justify. Even then, try to remember that emotion is your greatest enemy when it comes to making financial decisions—a fact we'll cover in detail in the next chapter.

Let me share a very quick story of a reverse mortgage gone wrong.

A client came into my office. Her mother, who had just died, had taken out a reverse mortgage on the family cabin because she didn't have enough money to meet her expenses in retirement. She needed the equity but never told the kids she had taken out the loan.

Now, the kids had always planned on either buying or inheriting this cabin, up in Minnesota lake country. They'd been going there as a family all their lives and loved spending time at such an idyllic retreat. They wanted to keep it in the family for the next generation.

But when my client's mom passed, the kids learned about the reverse mortgage by way of the bank, which told them they had to come up with the capital to pay it off very quickly, otherwise the cabin would be sold. The family couldn't pull together the funds to buy it and lost their getaway.

With a little planning and better communication, the kids could have bought that cabin from Mom while she was still alive. They would have not only kept it in the family but also given Mom the income she needed.

There is almost always a better alternative than a reverse mortgage, but I think there's an even bigger lesson in this story. The sooner you get a financial plan for retirement in place, the less likely it becomes that you'll have to sacrifice the things you've worked for all your life, in order to fund your retirement.

In this chapter, we've covered a broad range of options for establishing and growing your retirement savings. Cultivating a diverse mix of these vehicles can be a big key to overcoming your income gap. But the biggest key in bridging that gap—and in positioning yourself and your family for the future—is growing your retirement savings.

Investing your savings wisely is the surest way to do that, so let's turn to the psychology of investing and study the strategies that can best position yourself and your family for the future.

CHAPTER 6

INVESTMENT STRATEGIES TO BRIDGE YOUR INCOME GAP

"You don't need to be a rocket scientist. Investing is not a game where the guy with the 160 IQ beats the guy with 130 IQ."

—WARREN BUFFETT

The retirement savings tools covered in chapter 5 form the foundation of your retirement income, but the money you put in those vehicles, on its own, is not going to bridge your income gap. Growing your savings is the key, and investing is how that growth happens.

Investing. The word alone is enough to scare many people, but the previous quote from one of the greatest investors of all time is right on the money: successful investing is not rocket science. It does, however, require awareness of market volatility and self-control—specifically, knowing when to act and, even more important, when not to.

This chapter explores in great detail two areas I think are most crucial to achieving steady growth of your retirement savings: Investor behavior and market risk.

External factors and engrained human psychology too often lead us to make poor investment decisions. Understanding why we behave as we do is the first step in changing our behavior.

Market risk and how we manage it will largely determine whether our investment approach is strategic or scattershot. When it comes to growing your retirement savings, a strategic approach is always the better option.

Before we can enact a strategy, however, we must first understand the behaviors that result, for too many of us, in poor investment decisions.

OUR WORST ENEMY ON WALL STREET? OURSELVES

DALBAR, a research group that analyzes investment performance, has quantified the success of individual investors in growing their retirement accounts specifically. Their findings are stunning, as the chart on the adjacent page reveals.

The black bar tracks the historical ten-year average rate of return of the S&P 500. The gray bar shows the returns that average investors realized over those same time periods. In every case, the difference is dramatic.

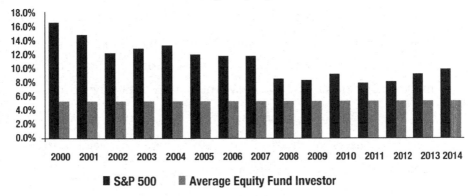

Going back twenty years from 2015, for example, the S&P 500 gained 9.58 percent, while the average investor made 5.19—a **difference of 4.39 percent. Nearly half!**

Why did these pending retirees' investments do so poorly? Fear and greed, the biggest drivers of bad investment decisions. If you're trying to build retirement savings, fear and greed, very simply, are your worst enemies—and they come from one place only: inside ourselves.

Looking back over time, the cyclical nature of the market is clear. That cycle has repeated again and again.

It begins when the market begins to see big gains, often on the strength of one particular economic sector. People then buy into that sector, more of them every day, without thinking much about fundamentals. They only see that share prices keep going up and want to get in on the prosperity.

It happened with the tech bubble of 1999 and the credit crisis of 2008: Before these market downturns, the smartest people in the world were making big financial decisions—based, like those of average investors, on fear and greed.

In both of those market calamities, the value of the "booming" economic sector was nowhere near the amount of money investors poured into it. Some people feared missing out. The greedy doubled down, trying to squeeze a little more money from an already-oversold market. Whichever emotion drove them, they kept buying in.

That creates bubbles, and sooner or later, bubbles burst.

What drives investor fear and greed? There are several sources—some external and some built into our psyches.

MEDIA

Perhaps the biggest external influence on investors is the media: TV, the Internet, and the twenty-four-hour news cycle they've created.

Just when we think an event has been reported from every conceivable angle, the news anchor looks solemnly into the camera and asks, "How will this impact the financial markets?" A Wall Street "expert" appears (he must be an expert because *he's* on *TV*, right?) expressing euphoria or doom and gloom. The next thing we know, we're buying or selling investments, when doing the opposite—or just leaving them alone—would be wiser.

Why do the media put everything under a microscope and hype the latest news as if it were—as the eighties hit song goes—"the end of the world as we know it"? It's simple; their primary goal is not helping *you* make money. It's ensuring that sure *they* do.

CNN, CNBC, Fox, and every media outlet are interested in one thing: ratings. The more viewers who tune in (or in the case of the Internet, the more views a website gets), the more advertising the outlet sells. The more advertising they sell, the more money they make, and the happier *their* shareholders become.

What's the surest way to keep people tuning and logging in? By sensationalizing every story and creating a connection—however implausible it may be—between the event and its potential impact on viewers.

Not long ago we had an Ebola scare in Africa. Soon after, worries about the Chinese economy. Both times, CNBC ran a special report, "Markets in Turmoil." Regular programming was canceled and somber, concerned "experts" were brought in because negative news gets more people to tune in.

Just like that, media-generated fear drove people to make rash financial decisions, and that's the effect every time, as this chart illustrates.

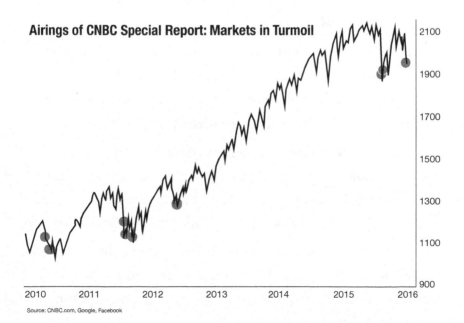

Airings of CNBC Special Report: Markets in Turmoil

Source: CNBC.com, Google, Facebook

If fear is the biggest factor in investor behavior, greed is a very close second. Exhibit A? *Mad Money*, the wildly popular CNBC show, hosted by Jim Cramer.

Cramer was a successful hedge fund manager. He's extremely smart, no question about it, and made a lot of money on Wall Street. But now, Cramer's pretty much a one-man media empire. He makes millions hosting *Mad Money* and writes for a website called TheStreet. com, which he founded and sold and from which he now draws a seven-figure salary. Cramer contributes to other CNBC shows and has written and recorded many books. But by far, *Mad Money* is his biggest brand.

The show itself is very entertaining. Cramer runs around the raucous set, high-fives people in the screaming audience, hypes certain stocks, takes viewer phone calls, and shouts "Booyah!" into the camera. It's great theater. Lots of people watch. Unfortunately, many also act on what Cramer says.

Unfortunately because what does he really know about viewers' personal situations—about their appetite for risk, how much they can afford to lose, how much income they need, the retirement they want, or how their other assets are currently invested?

Fun as it might be from an entertainment standpoint, *Mad Money* is about as far as you can get from personalized financial advice. Worse, Cramer feeds the notion that the show helps everyday investors. One of his books is actually called *Watch TV and Get Rich*.

That's absurd—and Cramer, while best known, is just one of the media's many financial "experts." Their on-air antics lead people to make investment decisions based on fear, greed, and hype—not on the reality of their personal situations.

FRIENDS AND FAMILY

If "experts" you've never met and who don't know the first thing about you are poor sources of financial advice, then what about friends, family, and coworkers?

You're at the water cooler on a coffee break—or maybe at lunch—with coworkers. Perhaps it's a neighborhood cookout or a holiday gathering with the family. The conversation turns to the stock market.

You know these people to one degree or another—but does their investing acumen warrant placing value in their advice? Do they have any better understanding of things than you do, or are they just quoting what they read somewhere, trying to make themselves sound smarter?

I work in the industry as an advisor, but that doesn't mean I know the first thing about the finances of my neighbors at a picnic table. It would be irresponsible of me to offer investment advice or stock tips without understanding someone's net worth, risk tolerance, and the other factors that go into a comprehensive financial plan.

Still, at gatherings with family or friends, someone will usually come up to me and say, "So-and-so said I should buy gold." I get it all the time, especially when the markets are volatile.

"Gold can be a safe haven when the markets are in crisis mode," I might say, "but overall, its value has dropped over the last several years." I'd rather not do this particular person a disservice by offering off-the-cuff advice, nor would I feel comfortable giving it.

Just like media experts, friends, family, and coworkers are going to be positive when the markets are up. They'll tell you to be more aggressive, to get a little greedier. When the markets get volatile, fear kicks in. They think maybe they were too aggressive and suggest you get more conservative too.

TV and Internet outlets sell advertising by getting you to watch or log on. The people at your neighborhood cookout are trying to sell you too—on the idea that they're sharing valuable insights.

All they're really doing, though, is killing time until the burgers are done. Are they the people you want to rely on for decisions affecting your financial future?

BEHAVIORAL FINANCE

Here's more sage advice from Warren Buffett: "Be fearful when others are greedy and greedy when others are fearful." That's truly how the market plays out. The worst time to invest is when there's no bad news. Many of us know this on some level, yet we ignore it. Why?

In addition to the external influences we've just studied, there are internal mechanisms at work. Human behavior and cognitive psychology play important roles in the financial choices we make.

In fact, an entire field called "behavioral finance" studies the tendencies rooted deep in our DNA as they relate to economics and finance, in an attempt to explain why people make irrational financial decisions. Behavioral finance has uncovered two main types of bias that may lead to decisions that don't line up logically with market trends: emotional and cognitive.

Emotional bias: Researchers Amos Tversky and Daniel Kahneman are widely credited with founding behavioral finance decades ago. Their research showed that financial losses are twice as powerful, psychologically, as gains.

This explains why, when people come into my office, I rarely hear how great their investments are doing. I hear about the losers. Research shows that people remember negative events much longer than positive ones.

Tversky and Kahneman's best-known contribution to this field of study is prospect theory. It earned Kahneman a Nobel Prize, and says people make decisions based on *potential* losses and gains (i.e., on their prospects)—and that they take *mental shortcuts* in doing so. Rather than weigh *all* the relevant information, people typically focus on information that portends a *positive* outcome.

For example, let's say you have a winning stock. You sell that stock quickly to take the gain, to get that good feeling of having *won*. Okay, but let's say you have a loser. Emotional bias makes it more likely you'll hold it because you don't want to suffer the *loss*. You convince yourself it will turn around. That's prospect theory in action. Giving greater weight to an attractive *possibility* than to facts that indicate a negative result.

Behavioral finance has also uncovered some **cognitive biases**, and several stand out in regard to investing: *recency bias, overconfidence, home bias*, and what I consider the biggest threat, *anchoring*.

With *recency bias,* we use past events to project future outcomes, regardless of their relevance. For example, telling yourself that if the market has gone up the past two years, it's bound to keep going up. Recency bias is making presumptions based on recent history, with no evidence to support them.

Overconfidence, of course, is when investors think they know more than they actually do. They invest on the belief that the market lacks the unique insight about some company that they've been able to discern, even though—and this is important—the market is always a couple of steps ahead of us. Unless you've got actual insider information, trust me, the "unique insight" you gained reading a financial blog or watching TV is already baked into that stock.

Home bias is one I see a lot here in Minnesota, home of 3M, one of the thirty largest corporations in the world. It's a great company, but many people buy local firms not because they're great investments but because they're local. Even daily market reports encourage home bias, don't they? "Checking stocks of local interest . . ."

These three cognitive biases exist in varying degrees, but *anchoring bias* is one of the most widespread and one that I see costing individual investors a lot of money.

Say a stock was once trading at $80, but today it's around $40. Many people will "anchor" their investing strategy to the higher number. They figure the company's a proven winner; it's bound to get back to its high.

But what if key fundamentals have changed? In that case, what the company *was* worth at some point in the past is meaningless. Here's an extreme example case.

A gentleman came into my office years ago and said he'd been a backhoe operator for Enron. I instantly knew his story was not going to end well.

(In case you're not familiar with the Enron scandal, there's a documentary film I highly recommend: *Enron: The Smartest Guys in the Room*. It shows what can happen when people make anchoring their investment strategy.)

Enron was a high-flying company in the energy sector. It was making millions and millions of dollars for shareholders, many of whom, like this backhoe operator, were company employees.

Enron sold stock to employees at a big discount. Workers could invest up to 25 percent of their earnings in company stock, also put their 401(k) money in Enron shares, *and* get a company match of *still more* Enron stock.

Before long, this backhoe operator had about $7 million in company stock, and he wasn't alone. Enron workers around the world built their retirement savings on company shares. They watched the price go up and up for years. When it began to drop, company executives said it was due to explosive growth and that share prices would recover.

Like many of his coworkers, the backhoe operator anchored. He said, "When the stock gets up to $100, I'll sell." Which would have been fine, if the price *had actually reached* $100.

As we now know, Enron was a huge Ponzi scheme, carried out by the very executives who promised workers that everything was fine. They were eventually convicted of fraud and conspiracy.

But in the moment—even as news surfaced about possible malfeasance—the backhoe operator kept believing everything would turn around. If he'd sold his shares at the first inkling of trouble, he would have had more than enough money to last his lifetime and to do whatever he wanted.

Along with thousands of other Enron employees, anchoring led him to ignore the outward signs of impending disaster. He kept lowering his "sell" target, convincing himself the stock would rally one more time—until he had less than $10,000 left.

SO WHAT'S THE RIGHT STRATEGY?

Clearly, outside influences and human psychology conspire in leading us to make bad investment decisions. That's why getting objective professional help is so important. It's the surest way to counter the emotional element each of us brings to our personal finances.

I do mean each of us—no one is immune. Though I work in the industry, when it comes to *my money*, I'm just as susceptible to emotional responses as any other investor.

As an advisor, however, my fiduciary responsibility to clients allows me to see and help them avoid big behavioral mistakes like those just described, which can utterly ravage one's assets over time.

In planning for retirement, that's really the key word: time.

As we're about to see, an investment strategy geared for the long term is more likely to withstand the market's inherent short-term volatility.

Back in chapter 1, I compared people who sell investment products without intimate knowledge of your situation to doctors who prescribe medication without diagnosing your illness—they're committing malpractice.

While a long-term investment strategy is the surest way to grow your retirement savings, what specific program of treatment—what investment "prescription"—is most likely to work *for you?*

WHAT ARE YOU WORKING WITH?

To start figuring that out, we need to look at your current holdings. Many people have accounts scattered all over the place: one or two 401(k)s over here, a couple of IRAs there, maybe a brokerage account as well.

You can't make investment decisions without knowing what you're working with. That means getting all your information in one place. You're going to draw retirement income from all those holdings at some point, but when your account information is scattered, putting together a comprehensive plan is difficult at best.

Once you've gathered all your information, it's time to analyze it.

If you own mutual funds, and many of us do, you're likely to find a lot of overlap within your investments. Owning ten different funds doesn't mean you're diversified. On closer inspection, you may find that half of them are heavy in, say, Apple stock. So you're at greater risk because your holdings, overall, are weighted toward Apple's performance.

Knowing what accounts you have and what they're already invested in is the first critical step in formulating a long-term investment strategy.

Taxes are another consideration.

For example, bonds are typically better owned inside a 401(k)-type plan or an IRA, because no matter how you take money out, it's taxed as ordinary income. Stocks, meanwhile, allow you to take advantage of the dividend tax rate, which is typically less for most people—so it's better to own stocks *outside* of a 401(k) or IRA. These are just a couple of quick examples; we'll look at tax issues much more closely in chapter 7.

What about liquidity? As a future retiree, you're going to take income at some point. Now's the time to start thinking about your time horizon, about when you'll start drawing on each of your accounts. Then you're ready to explore strategies that can provide the growth needed to help bridge your income gap.

INVESTING 101

Many of today's retirees think about investing in terms of their ratio of stocks to bonds. For many years, it was accepted wisdom: "As you get older, you should add more bonds and reduce stocks. You should become more conservative."

As we've seen, however, people are retiring earlier and living longer. To hit the brakes and mitigate future growth just to protect your savings a bit more could actually increase the odds that you'll run out of money in retirement. Understanding the traditional roles of stocks and bonds can help explain why their roles are now changing.

The stock market is volatile, even in positive years. It might average 9 or so percent over the long term, but in the shorter term there's volatility, known as "market risk." That risk is what prevents us from simply investing in stocks and happily making 9 percent, instantly and forever.

S&P 500 intra-year declines vs. calendar year returns

Despite average intra-year drops of 14.2%, annual returns positive in 27 of 36 years

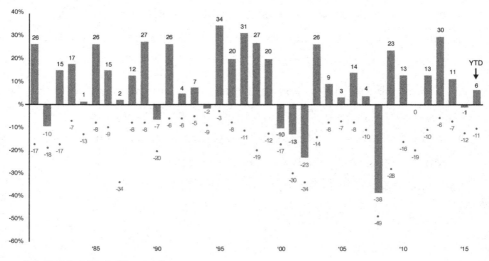

Source: FactSet, Standard & Poor's, J.P. Morgan Asset Management

As this chart illustrates, even when the market makes double-digit returns, there tends to be double-digit corrections within the same trading year.

In 2010, for example, the market finished up about 15 percent overall, but there was a 16 percent decline during the course of the year. Such strong volatility isn't typical, but in most years, a correction of 5 percent or more is common.

People want a hedge against that volatility, a safer place to put some of their savings but still get decent growth, while leaving a larger portion of their assets in the market to ride out its short-term turbulence. For many years, bonds were that safer haven.

Back in the 1980s, it was common for 20 to 40 percent of a portfolio to be invested in bonds. Much higher interest rates in those days allowed bonds to spin off nice dividends, interest, or coupon payments, helping investors to mitigate market volatility.

Today, however, interest rates are at historic lows. Bonds still have a place in diversifying and helping to protect your money, but they may not provide the cushion they did as recently as ten or fifteen years ago.

That's a basic change from what our parents and grandparents could expect—just like retirement itself is very different.

Remember our discussion of inflation in chapter 4? It's something we need to consider in our overall retirement planning strategy. If bonds were still that reliable place to park some assets and get decent returns, then their gains might offset inflation; they certainly did in prior generations. But in a 2012 interview with *Bloomberg News*, Warren Buffett called bonds the most dangerous asset class on inflation; he's no longer confident bonds can counter inflation's effects over time.[9]

I'm not suggesting you avoid bonds altogether, but to make a broader point, even as you implement your specific investment strategy, it's important to look at the larger economic picture along the way. An impartial professional advisor can suggest adjustments to strategy that may leverage changing trends to your advantage.

OTHER TYPES OF MARKET RISK

A sound investment strategy maximizes returns while minimizing risk. We just identified one of the three most dangerous types of market risk: *stock market volatility*. The other two are *sequence-of-returns risk* and *business risk*.

Even if you exceed your investment objectives, the larger trend in the market at the time you enter retirement can profoundly impact the income available to you as your retirement continues. That's *sequence-of-returns risk*. Though tied to stock market volatility, sequence-of-returns risk is unique in that it specifically impacts retirees. To adequately illustrate how this risk develops, we must first understand its relationship to a number featured in nearly every mutual fund or other investment prospectus, that investment's "average rate of return" (ARR).

ARR translates an investment's returns into an annual average, usually over a period of ten years or longer. Considering ARR along with other factors on the front end of a long-term investment

---

9 "Buffet Says Bonds Among Most Dangerous Assets on Inflation," Bloomberg, February 9, 2012, http://www.bloomberg.com/news/articles/2012-02-09/buffett-says-bonds-are-among-most-dangerous-assets-on-low-rates-inflation.

strategy can be helpful. Upon retirement, however, ARR becomes less important, and sequence-of-returns risk becomes a real threat.

To illustrate, imagine for a moment that the market gains 100 percent of its value in a single year and drops 50 percent the next year.

At the end of that two-year period, the market is right back where it started. But when you subtract the second year's 50 percent decline from the first year's 100 percent gain and divide the remaining 50 percent by the two years in the period—boom! The ARR for the period is 25 percent, suggesting the market gained in each year, even though your portfolio begs to differ.

One-year increases and declines like these have never happened. Still, the example shows how the market's short-term trend can impact us, even when we've followed a long-term investment strategy to prepare for retirement.

But, you're thinking, *my overall holdings haven't changed. What's the problem?*

Let's say you've just retired and need $5,000 from your portfolio. If the market is trending downward when you withdraw that money, then it is going to be much more difficult to replace it through market gains than it would be if the market was trending upward. To make matters worse, you've stopped contributing investment principal, since you're no longer earning it at work.

It can become a perfect storm. You're drawing on the assets you've carefully built up to fund your retirement, you're likely to continue doing so, you're not replacing it, and all this is happening as the market's downward trend is reducing your retirement savings' value.

Avoiding significant drawdowns in the early years of retirement is a big concern for retirees. Think about someone who retired in 2007, at the top of the market, never suspecting that the biggest market decline since the Great Depression was about to happen. Let's assume they had $1 million saved for retirement and were taking $40,000 a year for income. After the 2008 financial crisis, their $1 million in savings was suddenly $650,000, although their $40,000 income requirement stayed the same. That increased this hypothetical retiree's withdrawal rate from 4 percent to 6.15 percent, practically overnight. This is a high annual withdrawal rate that could potentially put the longevity of their retirement savings at risk.

The impact of sequence-of-returns risk is comparable to carrying a backpack full of rocks up a ladder. It can wear out your portfolio earlier in retirement, negatively impacting your capacity for growth as retirement continues.

The chart on the adjacent page illustrates the potential negative impact sequence-of-returns risk can produce on a portfolio.

Sequence-of-returns risk really drives home the importance of getting professional help with retirement planning. A trusted advisor will help you to determine your appetite for risk based on these types of considerations. Unfortunately, many investors do not feel the pain of taking too much risk until it is too late. Coupling that with taking withdrawals for income in retirement creates a sensitive situation for managing investment risk.

In addition to *stock market volatility* and *sequence-of-returns risk*, I look closely at *business risk*—having too much invested in a particular company—when advising clients on strategies for growing their retirement savings.

SEQUENCE-OF-RISK RETURNS

These tables depict equivalent average returns for Portfolios A and B, however, the table on the right depicts the sequence of returns while making distributions—a big difference!

| | Annual Income = None | | | | | Annual Income= 5% of first-year value adjusted thereafter for inflation | | | |
| | Starting Value for Portfolio A and Portfolio B = **$100,000** | | | | | Starting Value for Portfolio A and Portfolio B = **$684,848** | | | |
Age	Annual Return	Portfolio A Year-End Value	Annual Return	Portfolio B Year-End Value	Age	Annual Return	Portfolio A Year-End Value	Annual Return	Portfolio B Year-End Value
41	-12%	$87,695	29%	$129,491	66	-12%	$566,337	29%	$852,571
42	-21%	$69,426	18%	$152,281	67	-21%	$413,086	18%	$967,355
43	-14%	$59,707	25%	$189,590	68	-14%	$318,927	25%	$1,168,029
44	22%	$72,984	-6%	$178,404	69	22%	$352,432	-6%	$1,061,698
45	10%	$80,136,	15%	$204,272	70	10%	$348,431	15%	$1,177,105
46	4%	$83,595	8%	$221,183	71	4%	$323,772	8%	$1,234,855
47	11%	$92,707	27%	$281,124	72	11%	$318,176	27%	$1,528,614
48	3%	$95,210	-2%	$274,939	73	3%	$284,653	-2%	$1,452,871
49	-3%	$92,155	15%	$315,355	74	-3%	$232,143	15%	$1,623,066
50	21%	$111,507	19%	$375,272	75	21%	$236,215	19%	$1,886,771
51	17%	$130,129	33%	$498,737	76	17%	$229,644	33%	$2,461,500
52	5%	$137,026	11%	$554,097	77	5%	$194,417	11%	$2,687,327
53	-10%	$123,597	-10%	$499,795	78	-10%	$126,543	-10%	$2,375,148
54	11%	$137,316	5%	$526,284	79	11%	$90,304	5%	$2,450,746
55	33%	$182,493	17%	$614,174	80	33%	$68,219	17%	$2,808,226
56	19%	$217,167	21%	$743,150	81	19%	$27,833	21%	$3,344,606
57	15%	$249,091	-3%	$719,305	82	15%	$0	-3%	$3,182,338
58	-2%	$243,611	3%	$738,726	83	-2%	$0	3%	$3,211,664
59	27%	$309,629	11%	$819,247	84	27%	$0	11%	$3,503,440
60	8%	$335,262	4%	$854,602	85	8%	$0	4%	$3,594,592
61	15%	$383,875	10%	$938,354	86	15%	$0	10%	$3,885,017
62	-6%	$361,226	22%	$1,147,022	87	-6%	$0	22%	$4,685,257
63	25%	$449,727	-14%	$986,439	88	25%	$0	-14%	$3,963,710
64	18%	$528,878	-21%	$780,941	89	18%	$0	-21%	$3,070,398
65	29%	$684,848	-12%	$684,848	90	29%	$0	-12%	$2,622,984
	8%	$684,848	8%	$684,848		8%	$0	8%	$2,622,984

↖ **NO DIFFERENCE** ↗   ↖ **BIG DIFFERENCE** ↗

Total income generated by portfolio during retirement = $718,045 $1,248,438

In discussing *home bias* earlier in the chapter, I mentioned 3M. It's not uncommon for people here in Minnesota, where the company is based, to have 50 percent or more of their assets in that one company.

That's fine, if the company you're heavily invested in happens to be doing well when you retire. If it is not, however, the impact could be beyond significant. Which will be the case?

There's no sure way to know—and managing risk means minimizing uncertainty.

It's one thing to risk heavy investment in one company early in your career, when there's still time to recover. The closer you get to retirement, however, the more important it becomes to put your eggs in a variety of baskets.

THINK LONG TERM—AND DIVERSIFY

The best way to manage all these risks—each of which is associated with short-term market volatility—is through a good long-term investment strategy with diversification at its core. This chart shows why.

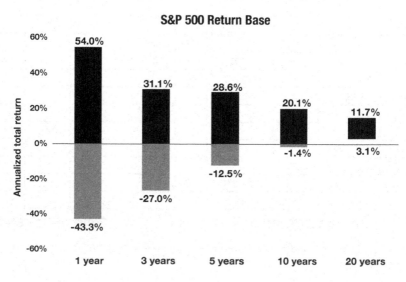

S&P 500 Return Base

Source: Charles Schwab

The chart breaks out the stock market's performance into one-, three- five-, ten- and fifteen-year periods, going back to 1926. Looking at those rolling periods across all that time, you had about a 75 percent chance that an investment in the broad market would see positive results within its first year. That's a crystal-clear indication of the market's *inherent* short-term volatility.

But look what happens three years in: 83 percent of the three-year periods were positive. It gets consistently better, until—at fifteen years—there's a nearly 100 percent certainty that you'll make money. Those are good odds by any standard.

The problem, as this chapter has shown, is that many investors react emotionally during periods of short-term market volatility— even though short-term volatility is the rule, not the exception! This chart's nearly one-hundred-year data set proves it!

It's really very simple. Investors who are trying to build retirement savings stand a much better chance of achieving their objectives through a long-term strategy than by trying to pick winners and jumping from one investment to another. That, however, is just the half of it.

The other half is diversification.

Serious risks come with investing too heavily in *any* one thing, whether a company, a particular economic sector, or an *asset class*.

Asset classes categorize investments by type: large cap, small cap, equity, high-yield, commodities, cash, real estate, etc. J.P. Morgan Asset Management tracks the performance of asset classes quarterly and aggregates the information to determine broader trends.

From 2005 to 2010, for example, real estate was the best asset class by far. Once the 2008 financial crisis hit, however, those early years proved meaningless. Real estate experienced greater volatility than any other asset class over those ten years. It was not the best time to be a retiree heavily invested in real estate, at least not one who values restful nights.

Cash was another interesting asset class during that decade. We tend to think of cash (i.e., savings) as a good place to be. While cash was stable across those ten years, it was also at or near the bottom of all asset classes in performance. In other words, it was flat.

Cash is fine, provided you have enough. Getting enough, however, requires saving—and investment.

Diversification and a long-term investment approach can achieve that growth. It's very hard to get "hurt" if your investments are spread across a range of asset classes, economic sectors and companies, and—as we've just seen—if you stay in the market for ten years or more.

We've covered a lot in this chapter, such as:

- ◎ the emotional and psychological influences that can lead to irrational investment decisions;

- ◎ how, like retirement itself, the "accepted wisdom" around investing has changed, thanks to new realities in the broader economy;

- ◎ key risks we must minimize in order to preserve our savings once we've stopped working; and most important

- ◎ how a strategy focused on long-term investing and diversification can grow retirement savings to help bridge our income gap.

Take some time to fully understand and digest this information. If you do, I'm confident that you'll begin to think about investing in a whole new light. Next, we'll turn to strategies for diversifying your various sources of retirement income in order to minimize your tax liability.

CHAPTER 7

TO MAXIMIZE RETIREMENT INCOME, MINIMIZE YOUR TAXES

"When a man retires, his wife gets twice the husband but only half the income."

—CHI-CHI RODRIGUEZ, PRO GOLFER (AND SEMI-PRO COMEDIAN)

nflation, life expectancy, various market risks, changing conditions in the broader economy—and, our focus in this chapter, taxes—can all increase your income gap. Without a strategy for addressing these realities, Chi-Chi's observation, while humorous, might also prove true.

Stress-testing is the key to devising a working retirement plan that keeps everybody happy. Testing your retirement against known and potential obstacles helps to identify approaches for overcoming those challenges.

We began the stress-testing process in chapter 4, by projecting

the expenses you'll face throughout retirement. Next, we explored options for establishing retirement savings and then learned the benefits of a common-sense, long-term investment strategy.

Now we turn to diversification, the surest way to preserve your hard-earned, carefully invested assets—and to protect them from unnecessary taxation.

WHY DIVERSIFY?

As we've already seen, your retirement savings can fall prey to a host of risks. Taxes, however, needn't be one of them. Diversifying your assets in a way that reduces your total tax liability may increase the income available to you in retirement. That, in turn, can help preserve your assets so they are not exhausted too quickly.

Minimizing your post-retirement tax liability also protects the gains your savings have achieved through investment. If you don't act to cut your taxes, then you could hand a significant share of those gains right to Uncle Sam.

Many retirees wind up paying higher taxes than necessary due to a combination of factors.

First, Americans are increasingly saving for retirement through tax-deferred vehicles. We save with pre-tax dollars because we've been conditioned to keep our taxes as low as possible.

So we put as much pre-tax income as we can in our 401(k)s or traditional IRAs and tend to forget—or ignore—that eventually we'll have to pay up! Distributions from these accounts in retirement, which we must begin taking when we turn age seventy and a half, will be taxed at "ordinary income" rates.

We might also have a pension. Its payouts will *also* be taxed at ordinary income.

Then there's Social Security—and up to 85 percent of *that* money could be taxed at ordinary income too!

But—we've been led to believe—that's okay because our retirement income will be so much lower than while we were working. That *might* be true, but the deductions you were able to claim while working might decrease as well. If you've paid off your house, then you'll no longer have a mortgage interest deduction. If your children are grown, then you'll lose that deduction too.

In truth, you might have *more* taxable income in retirement than you'd imagined and lack deductions to offset it.

Tax-deferred retirement accounts force us to take money out whether we need it or not, increasing our taxable income and explaining why many people become frustrated with their financial picture a few years into retirement. The taxes they've avoided for years are coming due, and for many, the "hit" is higher than expected. They're effectively trapped.

Fortunately, it's possible to create some tax flexibility. That's because different retirement savings vehicles carry one of three different tax liabilities: *currently taxable, tax-deferred,* or *tax-exempt.*

One of my goals as a financial advisor is to help clients hold their total federal tax liability in retirement at or below 15 percent if possible. I do it by diversifying their retirement savings across the tax-liability spectrum. Doing so can help many retirees avoid the postretirement tax trap.

THREE TAX BUCKETS

Picture three buckets of money.

Your *currently taxable* savings in Bucket #1 should be staked to non-qualified accounts. These include brokerage and investment accounts and checking and savings accounts.

Gains accruing to these accounts through the purchase and sale of stocks, bonds, or mutual funds will subject to either long- or short-term capital gains taxes; it depends on how long you own each investment. If under a year, you'll pay the short-term rate, which can be substantial: 10 to 39.6 percent, based on your ordinary income tax rate.

Non-qualified interest income is *also* taxed at ordinary income tax rates, interest on a corporate bond, for example. To be tax efficient, it may be better to hold items subject to ordinary income tax in other buckets—more on that in a moment.

Because issues you intend to hold more than a year are taxed at the long-term capital gains rate, keeping them in this bucket can prove more tax efficient. The long-term rate is much lower for most people, ranging from 0 to 20 percent. So—provided you've held each item in this bucket at least a year before selling it—you'll minimize the tax "hit."

Bucket #2 is for *tax-deferred* retirement savings: a 401(k), traditional IRA, or certain annuities.

You've likely paid no taxes on any of the money here. That reduced your taxable income while you worked. This bucket is a good place to hold issues that would otherwise be subject to short-term gains taxes—because they won't be subject to them here. As we've already seen, Uncle Sam charges only ordinary income tax rates on these accounts, provided you meet the age requirements for withdrawing money from them.

Bucket #3 is for *tax-exempt* retirement savings, money you've contributed to a Roth IRA from your after-tax income. (Some employers offer Roth 401(k)-type plans, which are subject to the same rules.) Like Bucket #2, this is a good place for more-frequently traded issues. In fact, it's perhaps the best place.

That's because, provided you've owned your Roth plan at least five years, you can draw on the principal *and the appreciation* it earns through investment, tax and penalty free, anytime after you turn fifty-nine and a half. And with no RMDs, there's no obligation to draw funds when you don't need them. This allows you to plan withdrawals in a way that may reduce your tax liability.

For example, at this writing (in 2016), federal income tax rates increase from 15 to 25 percent at $75,301 of income (married, filing jointly). A prudent strategy would be to withdraw from IRA accounts (Bucket #2) up to that limit, then switch to Roth IRAs (Bucket #3) and/or long-term capital gains and dividend income (Bucket #1).

Can you see how diversifying your assets across these buckets might limit your total federal tax liability in retirement to 15 percent? The key is to understand which investment types to place in each bucket based on your personal risk tolerance, retirement savings picture, and goals. I strongly recommend you get the help of a qualified financial advisor to ensure proper diversification, but let's look at some basic ideas.

STRESS TEST:

MAKE THE MOST OF SOCIAL SECURITY

As you stress-test your retirement plan against factors like living expenses, longevity, and lifestyle, Social Security could prove an important factor in helping to fill your income gap. The biggest question I get about Social Security, by far, is "When should I claim it?"

The short answer is "it depends."

The factors influencing this decision range from your other sources of retirement income to how long you anticipate living to your marital status. In short, there are no pat answers—but there are some basic rules of thumb that will help maximize the income you'll get as a Social Security recipient.

First and foremost: The longer you expect to live, the more advantageous waiting to claim your benefit tends to be. We covered this in some detail in chapter 5.

Second, remember that, as a tax-deferred retirement asset, your Social Security benefit resides in Bucket #2, meaning it is subject to income tax. Whether none, some, or most of that money is actually taxed depends on something called your provisional income.

Provisional income is the sum of your adjusted gross income, plus half of your Social Security benefit, plus any tax-exempt interest you collect on other assets (municipal bonds, for instance).

If you are married, file your taxes jointly, and your provisional income is under $44,000, 50 percent of your Social Security benefit will be subject to income tax, versus 85 percent if you're above that total. (Note that these are not tax *rates* but *percentages* of your Social Security benefit that are subject to tax.) Keep provisional income under $32,000 and you'll pay no income tax on your Social Security benefit at all. Single filers get similar considerations, with provisional income limits adjusted for their "solo" filing status.

Other strategies can affect Social Security's impact on your income gap.

If you claim Social Security at age sixty-two, limits on what you can earn from continued employment take effect. Exceed them and your Social Security benefit will be reduced. Contrary to popular belief, however, that money is not lost forever; it is added onto the benefit you'll receive at full retirement age.

Further, in the month that you attain full retirement age, limits on your income are uncapped. You can earn all you want without any reduction to your Social Security benefit.

These are especially important facts for folks claiming Social Security before full retirement age for fear that the program will run out of money. I just don't see that happening in the near term, and recent congressional action is one reason why.

While there's no doubt that further changes will be necessary if Social Security is to continue providing retirement benefits to future generations, the Bipartisan Budget Act of 2015 (BBA) was a first—and profound—step. I expect its changes to be the only significant ones affecting those who retire within the next decade.

The BBA closed two little-used loopholes that the Social Security Administration (SSA) feared would cost the program significant money, as large numbers of baby boomers retired and word of the loopholes spread. Just two-tenths of 1 percent of Social Security recipients were using them, but SSA considered both loopholes—known as *claim then suspend* and *spouse before worker*—"aggressive claiming" tactics that threatened the program's fiscal health.

Under the BBA, the *claim then suspend* loophole was closed immediately. *Spouse before worker* remains available to people who reached age sixty-two before January 2, 2016, and met other conditions. If you are in that group, spouse before worker (also called "restricted application") *might* provide you with additional income in retirement. Whether it will rests on a host of factors, and many "experts" have attempted to outline them in newspapers, magazines, and Internet postings since the BBA's enactment—only to prompt further questions from confused readers.

In fact, NPR and other news organizations have reported that customer service reps at SSA *itself* have dispensed inaccurate information about the BBA's effects, in phone conversations with pending retirees.

Clearly, the BBA and other factors in deciding when to claim Social Security are complex, so I won't put your financial future at risk by trying to generalize information that really must considered on a case-by-case basis.

Instead, I urge you to sit down with a trusted, professional financial advisor. Considering the when and how of claiming Social Security benefits within the context of your overall retirement plan is really the only way to understand—and maximize—the benefits you've earned and to which you are entitled.

PUTTING THE BUCKETS TO WORK

I'm going to describe here what I believe to be the best types of investments to hold in various accounts, but please note, proper asset allocation depends entirely on *your personal risk tolerance.* Your comfort with any investment strategy always trumps asset allocation!

Note too that these suggestions are based solely on tax liability. I urge you to work directly with a professional who understands and honors your risk tolerance before making any decisions about specific investment products.

Your *currently taxable* brokerage account—Bucket #1, funded with after-tax income—is the place to hold stocks that pay regular dividends. Though you'll pay tax on the dividend income every year, that rate, for most people, is just 15 percent.

Gains in the stocks *themselves* are not taxed—provided, of course, that you haven't sold them at a profit. Even if you do—provided you've held them at least one year—the rate will be lower than ordinary income tax.

The *tax-deferred* accounts in Bucket #2, where you save for retirement with pre-tax dollars, are tailor-made for trading short-term investments of less than a year's duration.

The traditional IRA and/or 401(k)-type plans in this bucket can't be depleted by capital gains taxes on the investment growth they achieve, so you can consolidate those gains year over year. When you start taking distributions in retirement, these savings will be taxed at ordinary income (and you'll face hefty penalties if you withdraw funds before you turn age fifty-nine and a half).

Bucket #2 is also the place for interest-paying bonds. Investment interest will be taxed at ordinary income whether held here or in your brokerage account, but here it grows tax-deferred—just like short-term investment growth—until you draw it out in retirement.

On to Bucket #3: the *tax-exempt* Roth bucket.

Growth-oriented stocks presenting the opportunities for long-term appreciation are typically best held here, where that growth potential can be maximized. The principal you contribute to a Roth account has already been taxed. If you're able to see good growth over the long term, it's best to earn it within an account that the IRS has no future claim on, right?

Let's summarize the basics of tax-based asset diversification:

- ◎ Bucket #1 holds *currently taxable*, nonqualified accounts to take advantage of long-term capital gains taxes and dividend tax rates.

- ◎ Bucket #2 contains *tax-deferred* retirement accounts like traditional IRAs and 401(k)s. It's the place to trade more frequently in order to avoid short-term capital gains taxes and to hold interest-bearing bonds. Upon retirement, withdrawals are taxed at ordinary income.

- ◎ Bucket #3 is your *tax-exempt* Roth IRA or Roth 401(k)-type plan. Investments within these accounts should attempt to maximize growth, since withdrawals in retirement are tax-free.

Properly balancing your assets among these three buckets offers the opportunity to distribute tax liability more efficiently in retirement. But what if your savings, at present, are in only one or two buckets?

No worries; there are strategies for balancing out your assets.

PUTTING BUCKS IN EVERY BUCKET

If you're like most Americans, it's probable that all of your retirement savings are in Bucket #2: tax-deferred accounts, like a company-funded pension, employer-sponsored 401(k), or traditional IRA.

Let's figure you've got an IRA and a couple of traditional 401(k)-type plans from former employers.

Maybe you've also invested in the stock market somewhat, with maybe $10,000 in Bucket #1, a brokerage account.

Hmmmm. No tax-exempt bucket. What's the best way to create one?

Let's assume that you're fifty-eight years old. Drawing money from your traditional IRA would really cost you. Since you haven't attained the minimum age of fifty-nine and a half for taking withdrawals, so you owe taxes on any withdrawal, *plus* a 10 percent penalty for taking it early. If you boost the withdrawal to help pay the penalty, then you'll pay still more taxes *and* the penalty on *that money too!*

No thanks!

What if you could convert funds from your traditional IRA to a Roth? You could leave those old 401(k)s in Bucket #2 and establish Bucket #3 as a new Roth account.

That's exactly what *Roth conversions* allow you to do, and over the last decade, they've become increasingly popular.

In 2010, the IRS made a monumental change. It did away with income limits for people converting traditional IRAs to Roth IRAs. Before the change, high-income earners could not do conversions;

the IRS didn't want to give up the revenue it would receive from those high-value accounts when their owners retired.

But in 2010, the government needed tax revenue badly, thanks to the lingering effects of the 2008 financial crisis. By dropping the income limit, Uncle Sam got the needed injection of revenue. High-income earners clamored to convert their traditional IRAs, happily paying tax at ordinary income in exchange for what would become substantial, tax-free, lifelong income for themselves and their families.

Unfortunately, that 10 percent early withdrawal penalty is now back in force. So, is the tax hit you'll incur with a Roth conversion worth the tax-free income it will provide in retirement?

To help you decide, remember two rules.

First: *You must pay taxes at ordinary income on the full amount being converted.*

Ideally, you want to pay the taxes from *other sources* to retain the larger conversion value of your new Roth. If you instead withhold the taxes from the amount converted, please note, pre- and post-age-fifty-nine, withdrawal rules apply! If you are younger than fifty-nine and a half, then you will pay a 10 percent penalty on the taxes withheld.

Second, *you must own each Roth conversion for five years in order to avoid the 10 percent early withdrawal penalty on the account's appreciation.*

If you are doing the conversion before the age of fifty-nine and a half again, these rules mean it's wiser to pay the taxes on the converted funds from *other sources*. If you take the money from the new Roth account, you'll pay the 10 percent early withdrawal penalty. People older than fifty-nine and a *half* can immediately tap their converted principal penalty free, but even then, using other sources is preferable. Why reduce your new Roth's investment principal right out of the gate?

Provided it is done correctly, a Roth conversion creates a tax-exempt bucket just when you need it most—as you explore options for minimizing taxes on the income you'll draw during retirement. A professional financial advisor can help you to navigate this complex process and establish what can become an important tool in your tax-reduction arsenal.

Another good interim step as you near retirement is rolling your old 401(k)-type plans into a traditional IRA. This can be critically important to the financial planning process, when you're putting together a retirement income strategy.

Beyond getting those funds out of your former employers' plans and into your own name with more control, a IRA rollover may provide you with better investment options than many 401(k)s.

STRESS TEST

IS NUA RIGHT FOR YOU?

My practice here in Minnesota is just down the road from one of the largest companies in the world: 3M. Not only does 3M provide fantastic benefits to employees, but its stock has also experienced great performance over the last few decades—so much that 3M matches the contributions of participants in its traditional 401(k) with company stock.

A stock that consistently returns nice gains is terrific, right? Sure. But it's important to remember that assets in a traditional 401(k) reside in Bucket #2. They will be taxed at ordinary income rates when you begin drawing on them in retirement.

If your 401(k) includes a lot of company stock, then you could forfeit significant gains to the IRS—unless you take advantage of something called net unrealized *appreciation (NUA)*.

	TAX RATE	TAXABLE AMOUNT	FEDERAL INCOME TAX OWED
NUA METHOD			
Cost basis of company stock	25%	$100,000	$25,000
NUA gain on stock sale	15%	$300,000	$45,000
Full IRA distribution	25%	$600,000	$150,000
		Total Tax Owed	$220,000

	TAX RATE	TAXABLE AMOUNT	FEDERAL INCOME TAX OWED
TRADITIONAL ROLLOVER			
Rollover full balance to IRA	25%	$1,000,000	$250,000
		Income tax savings using NUA	$30,000

As its name suggests, NUA is the total (net) gain (appreciation) on that stock, which you have not yet withdrawn (realized). A stock's NUA is the difference between its original value when you acquired it—called its "cost basis"—and its value when you sell it.

By following a very specific process, you can reduce your tax liability on the NUA of your company stock. Here's how it works.

John is sixty-three years old. He has $1 million in his 401(k), $400,000 of which is in the form of company stock. The stock's cost basis is $100,000, for an NUA of $300,000.

At retirement, John tells his 401(k) administrator that he wants to do an NUA transfer of his 401(k)'s assets. The $400,000 in company shares goes to a brokerage account (Bucket #1). The remaining $600,000 is rolled into an IRA. John maintains tax deferral (Bucket #2) on that portion.

John receives a 1099 at the end of the year for the $100,000 cost basis of company stock. He will owe—for *that year*—$25,000 in ordinary income tax on that money. (For clarity, I'm assuming John is in the 25 percent federal tax bracket, and leaving state taxes out of this example). But what happens, tax wise, to the $300,000 of NUA? That's the real beauty of this strategy.

Let's say John immediately sells all the stock and takes that gain. The long-term capital gains status of the stock *moves with it* to his brokerage account—which, for someone in the 25 percent federal bracket, means it will be taxed at just 15 percent.

If John left the 401(k) alone and drew everything from it over the course of his retirement, then he'd be taxed at 25 percent across the board, a total liability of $250,000. By paying 15 percent on the $300,000 of (now-realized) appreciation, he reduces that total to $220,000, a $30,000 savings. That's not pocket money!

The NUA strategy applies only to stock from an employer and requires a *full distribution* of 401(k) assets within the same tax year. It's not the right strategy for everyone, so be sure to consider it in terms of your broader financial plan.

DOING ROLLOVERS RIGHT

401(k) rollovers are a critical mechanism in the tax-based diversification of your retirement savings, so let's look at them a bit more closely.

When you leave an employer, whether for retirement or other opportunities—you really have three choices regarding the retirement savings you've amassed while working there.

First, the employer makes the check payable to you, and you're responsible for depositing that money into an IRA within sixty days, to preserve the tax-deferred status of those funds.

It sounds simple, but think twice before taking this route.

The reason? Getting that check in your own name automatically triggers your employer (or the plan administrator) to issue a 1099, showing it as taxable income. On your tax return, you must prove the funds went into an IRA within sixty days of receiving them.

That might seem like no big deal, but I'd rather eliminate any paperwork that might prompt the IRS to audit you, or just double-check your work.

There are two much better options, versions of what's called a "direct rollover."

I do 401(k) rollovers for clients all the time. Which one we use depends on how the 401(k) is administered.

If administered by the employer in-house, we have the check made payable to the new IRA's custodian. The employer might send it to the former employee or their custodian directly, but either way the employee is not the payee. This avoids potential tax conflicts and makes the process seamless, eliminating the need to prove the money is not taxable.

The second type of direct rollover is a transfer. It's essentially the same thing, but for plans managed by a third party. The plan administrator sends the money directly to the new IRA's custodian.

To ensure that your rollover is done correctly, I urge you to get help from your financial advisor. Since rollovers typically cannot be undone, mistakes can cost you.

For example, if the check used to convey the funds was made payable to you instead of to the appropriate entity, it could trigger a 20 percent mandatory withholding. If you were trying to transfer $100,000, you'd get a check for $80,000 and would have to come up with that tax hit of $20,000 on your own. If you're not yet age fifty-nine and a half, then the 10 percent early withdrawal penalty would also apply.

Any transaction involving a 401(k)-type plan that the IRS suspects wasn't done properly, based on the documentation, triggers taxes and penalties and places the burden for proving it was done right on your shoulders. Better to get help and get it right the first time, don't you think?

There are a few life circumstances when the IRS allows you to take money from your 401(k) or other tax-deferred account penalty free. We'll cover these exceptions later, but I strongly discourage my clients from using them unless there is simply no other option. Retirement accounts exist for your future. Early withdrawals can quickly short-circuit your financial plan.

STRESS TEST

IS AN ANNUITY RIGHT FOR YOU?

In chapter 5, I said annuities are a potential tool for saving toward retirement and regulating the income we take from those savings. Annuities are not growth vehicles in the purest sense, however, so it's important to understand how they may (or may not) help diversify your retirement assets to overcome your income gap.

Sold by insurance companies, annuities are sort of like pensions. Instead of an employer funding them, however, you do. You buy an annuity with your own money with a series of payments or a lump sum. In return, you get guaranteed payouts, income in each year of your retirement.

The amount you receive depends on what type of annuity you buy and factors you'd expect insurance companies to be concerned with: your age, health, life expectancy, and what sort of guaranteed payment you want.

Three types of annuities offer growth components: *fixed, variable,* and *fixed-indexed:*

◎ *Fixed annuities* are like certificates of deposit from a bank. Your money earns a guaranteed interest rate over a specific period of time. Unlike a CD, annuity interest grows tax deferred, and the term is usually longer.

◎ *Variable annuities* have been the most-sold type in recent years, and offer purchasers the broadest range of investment options. The payments you make are invested in sub-accounts (similar to mutual funds) you choose. This type of annuity has a variety of additional benefits that can be selected. These are often referred to as riders. Riders can range anywhere from providing a death benefit to some type of guaranteed income payout. The benefits are complex and vary from one insurance company to the next. I encourage you to do lots of research in advance.

◎ *Fixed-indexed* annuities are hybrids of the first two types. Returns are tied to the performance of a given stock market index—the Dow Jones index, for example. You typically don't choose specific investments. Due to the more conservative nature of these types of annuities, protection of principal and guaranteed income are the most common objective in using this type of vehicle.

◎ A fourth type of annuity offers no growth component. Called an *immediate annuity*, it requires a lump-sum payment—say, $100,000. It pays guaranteed income every year, right away. The payout depends on your age and life expectancy, and when you die the payments stop, with no cash value remaining.

Compared to the first three, immediate annuities are the most pension-like. You're betting that you'll live *x* number of years. If you do, you win the bet—keep winning, getting that same annual payout, until you die. If you die sooner, the insurance company "wins."

Annuities can reside in Bucket #1 or #2 because they carry the same options of tax-deferred or tax-free income as other retirement savings tools. It depends how you fund them. They also offer a host of guarantees, options for how and to whom payouts are made.

The biggest mistake I see current and soon-to-be retirees making with annuities is assuming they need one. Though annuities are heavily marketed as "must haves," a 2013 study by the Gallup Organization found that, of the 84 percent of baby boomers who purchase annuities for the guaranteed income they offer, only half end up using them.[10]

That's a whole lot of money insurance companies are keeping in their corporate coffers. It suggests that many people might do better by investing the money they are committing to annuities directly into the market instead. Here's why.

Imagine going to a racetrack. Before you place your bet, you head to the paddock to see the horses. They look pretty much the same in size, weight, and muscle structure. They all have jockeys that weigh 100, maybe 105 pounds. But then one enters the paddock with a guy six-foot-five and weighing in at 220 up top.

That's how annuities—especially *variable annuities*, the most popular type—compare to directly investing your money. You begin at a disadvantage. Since your purchase helps the insurance company make a profit on these products, growth alone isn't reason enough to buy one. A guaranteed, reliable annual chunk of income each year in retirement, however, may be enough for *some* people.

The trick, of course, is figuring out whether you're one of them.

---

10 The Gallup Organization, "2013 Survey of Owners of Individual Annuity Contracts," https://www.annuity-insurers.org/wp-content/uploads/2013/10/2013-Gallup-Survey.pdf.

Whole books have been written about annuities, so that's not a question I'll try to answer in the confines of this chapter. To best gauge whether an annuity is right for you, sit down with a professional advisor and review your retirement income projections. In the meantime, to avoid buying something you might not need, bear two things in mind: annuities may not offer the best potential for principal growth, but annuities may protect your money and may help fill your income gap.

THE IMPORTANCE OF TAX–BASED DIVERSIFICATION: JOHN AND JANE

Now that we've explored the basics of tax-based retirement asset diversification, it might be helpful to see how failing to properly spread your assets among the different tax buckets can widen, rather than reduce, your income gap.

Spouses John and Jane are both sixty-four years old, and their financial picture is one I see fairly often. They've just retired and will claim Social Security at age sixty-six. During their careers, they've accumulated $1 million in tax-deferred IRA and 401(k)-type accounts.

Their combined benefits from Social Security will provide $52,800 annually, and I've applied an annual inflation factor of 1.5 percent to those dollars, lower than the average of 2.26 percent in COLAs (cost-of-living increases) that Social Security has paid recipients over the past two decades.

As you'll recall from chapter 5, I have some concerns about Social Security. The numbers are just not adding up. I'm worried that it might therefore reduce its annual COLAs, so I am factoring that concern into my inflation projection of 1.5 percent.

In addition to couple's Social Security payments, Jane will receive a pension of $20,000 a year. This graphic shows their financial picture, beginning now and progressing through retirement.

John and Jane Smith

Retire at 64, Social Security at 66

Social Security, John $28,800 or $2400/mo.

Social Security, Jane $24,000 or $2,000/mo.

Pension, Jane $20,000/yr.

COLA=1.5%

Notes: Tax deductions not included.

	Income Needs	Pension	Social Security	Total Income	Taxable Income	Income Gap	Tax	After-Tax Income Gap
1	$60,000.00	$20,000		$20,000.00	$20,000	($40,000.00)	$2,073	($42,073)
2	$61,800.00	$20,000		$20,000.00	$20,000	($41,800.00)	$2,073	($43,873)
3	$63,654.00	$20,000	$52,800	$72,800.00	$64,880	$9,146.00	$8,805	342
4	$65,563.62	$20,000	$53,592	$73,592.00	$65,553	$8,028.38	$8,905	($877)
5	$67,530.53	$20,000	$54,396	$74,395.88	$66,236	$6,865.35	$9,008	($2,143)
6	$69,556.44	$20,000	$55,212	$75,211.82	$66,930	$5,655.37	$9,112	($3,457)
7	$71,643.14	$20,000	$56,040	$76,040.00	$67,634	$4,396.86	$9,218	($4,821)
8	$73,792.43	$20,000	$56,881	$76,880.60	$68,349	$3,088.16	$9,325	($6,237)
9	$76,006.20	$20,000	$57,734	$77,733.80	$69,074	$1,727.60	$9,434	($7,706)
10	$78,286.39	$20,000	$58,600	$78,599.81	$69,810	$313.42	$9,544	($9,231)
11	$80,634.98	$20,000	$59,479	$79,478.81	$70,557	($1,156.17)	$9,656	($10,812)
12	$83,054.03	$20,000	$60,371	$80,370.99	$71,315	($2,683.04)	$9,770	($12,453)
13	$85,545.65	$20,000	$61,277	$81,276.56	$72,085	($4,269.10)	$9,885	($14,154)
14	$88,112.02	$20,000	$62,196	$82,195.70	$72,866	($5,916.32)	$10,002	($15,919)
15	$90,755.38	$20,000	$63,129	$83,128.64	$73,659	($7,626.74)	$10,121	($17,748)
16	$93,478.04	$20,000	$64,076	$84,075.57	$74,464	($9,402.48)	$16,651	($26,054)
17	$96,282.39	$20,000	$65,037	$85,036.70	$75,281	($11,245.68)	$16,855	($28,101)
18	$99,170.86	$20,000	$66,012	$86,012.25	$76,110	($13,158.60)	$17,063	($30,221)
19	$102,145.98	$20,000	$67,002	$87,002.44	$76,952	($15,143.55)	$17,273	($32,417)
20	$105,210.36	$20,000	$68,007	$88,007.47	$77,806	($17,202.89)	$17,487	($34,689)
21	$108,366.67	$20,000	$69,028	$89,027.59	$78,673	($19,339.09)	$17,703	($37,042)
22	$111,617.67	$20,000	$70,063	$90,063.00	$79,554	($21,554.67)	$17,923	($39,478)
23	$114,966.20	$20,000	$71,114	$91,113.94	$80,447	($23,852.26)	$18,147	($41,999)
24	$118,415.19	$20,000	$72,181	$92,180.65	$81,354	($26,234.54)	$18,373	($44,608)
25	$121,967.65	$20,000	$73,263	$93,263.36	$82,274	($28,704.28)	$18,603	($47,308)
			$74,362					

Taxable Income	Marginal Tax Rate	Base Tax
$0-$18,550	10%	$1,855
$18,551-$75,300	15%	$10,368
$75,301-$151,900	25%	$29,518
$151,901-$231,450	28%	$51,792

Clearly, in those first two years, John and Jane have a fairly sizable income gap because they haven't yet claimed Social Security. This is a big reason people save money in Bucket #2 for so long; tax-deferred retirement accounts can help fill that void.

In the first year of retirement, John and Jane need $60,000 but only have $20,000 of income guaranteed at that point, from Jane's pension. So their income gap is $40,000 initially, and that doesn't account for taxes.

Jane's pension payouts are fully taxable. Based on current tax rates, the hit is about $2,073, increasing their first-year income gap to more than $42,000. They can bridge that with 401(k) funds—and probably will—but those too will be taxed at ordinary income.

Fast-forward two years. Social Security has kicked in, and things look better—at first.

John and Jane have $72,800 of income and only $63,654 of inflation-adjusted expenses for what looks like a surplus of just over $9,000. But again, here's where taxes can make things kind of get ugly for retirees.

Under current (2016) federal income tax laws, they'll pay $8,805, shrinking the surplus to $342. This is why tax planning—diversifying your retirement savings to minimize taxes and, in so doing, boost your income—becomes so important.

Let's look ten years into retirement. John and Jane are now seventy-four years old. Their income needs are a little over $78,000, the same amount they have coming in—before those pesky taxes, that is, which have also increased. John and Jane's income gap is now $9,231. If we look even further into their retirement, the increases become exponential.

When John and Jane's income exceeded $75,300, their tax rate jumped—from 15 to 25 percent (at current rates), excluding any deductions. That's big; 10 percent investment returns, which might make up that difference, are not easy to come by. Combine the higher tax bracket with the lack of deductions we discussed earlier—John and Jane have paid off their house, and the kids are long gone—and it's pretty clear why their income gap is expanding.

All these are critical considerations when doing your financial plan and show why spreading your assets across all three tax buckets is so important. Many Americans put the bulk of their retirement savings in Bucket #2, with tax-deferred retirement plans. Often, it's where they put everything.

As this chapter has shown, tax-exempt income from a Roth IRA (Bucket #3) can help offset the impact of the tax hit looming in Bucket #2. Similarly, long-term holdings in Bucket #1 can have a mitigating effect. The upshot is a lower overall tax liability (also known as your effective tax rate).

Whether your retirement income is less or more than John and Jane's, establishing holdings in Bucket #3 is prudent. It can reduce the RMDs you take from Bucket #2 and the tax bills that come with them, while Roth accounts have no RMDs and the money you withdraw is never taxed.

The importance—and complexity—of tax planning is difficult to overstate. Taxes can be a big contributor to your retirement income gap. We've explored the nuts and bolts in some detail, but the considerations and variables are just too numerous for any one book.

A trusted professional financial advisor can structure a plan that ensures your retirement savings are properly diversified. This can significantly reduce your tax liability—and increase the income available to you in retirement.

CHAPTER 8

INSURANCE: KNOW WHAT YOU NEED

"There are worse things in life than death. Have you ever spent an evening with an insurance salesman?"

—WOODY ALLEN

Most of us can relate to this quote. But have you ever stopped to wonder why?

The insurance industry is often ridiculed because it seems some folks who sell insurance are only interested in making a commission, while whether you actually need what they're selling is secondary. I have a different take.

Like every other profession, the insurance industry has agents who are a little too gung-ho and maybe not as interested in your needs as they should be—but I've found them to be the exception, not the rule.

Many of us buy insurance out of a sense of responsibility to the important people in our lives. Its true role, though, is to protect not just those people but also our other interests. The right policy can prevent catastrophic events from draining our assets.

A good insurance agent will respect your knowledge of your own situation and work closely with you to create the right coverage. The first step is identifying your needs—your greatest areas of vulnerability.

CHANGING PRIORITIES

Various things gain and lose importance at different points in our lives. When we're young, insuring a car, a home, and having good medical insurance for ourselves and our family are prominent concerns.

As we near retirement, the focus shifts. We've spent a lifetime building the two assets we're counting on see us through the rest of our lives: earning power and physical well-being. As we age, the chances increase that both will diminish. If they do, the cost—of a long-term disability, major medical procedure, or hospitalization—can at minimum reduce and at worst decimate the assets we've worked so hard to build.

To protect ourselves and those close to us from such catastrophic losses, there are four types of insurance I recommend considering: *disability, health, long-term care,* and *life.* Each type will hold a different priority for different people, but all can play important, protective roles as we face the realities that come with getting older.

DISABILITY INSURANCE

As we age, there's an increased chance that we'll become disabled. If an illness or injury is severe enough to limit or end your ability to work, you could be forced to draw on retirement savings much earlier than you imagined.

Some say, "I'd just go on worker's compensation." It's important to remember, though, that worker's comp only covers incidents that occur *on the job*. Wages lost due to that biking or skiing mishap are another story.

The disability provision of Social Security may help, but not today or tomorrow—perhaps not even this year. Approval often takes twelve months, sometimes longer. Assuming your appeal is eventually granted, it typically takes another month or two before checks appear in your mailbox.

That's a long time to be without income, but *disability insurance* can fill the void.

A prime feature of disability policies is that they quickly verify your eligibility for benefits. That means payments start quickly too.

Some employers include disability insurance in employee benefits packages. If yours isn't one of them, then you can buy coverage yourself. The goal is keep your household's income as close to the pre-injury (or illness) amount as possible, so your household's main income earner is usually the best candidate for a policy.

As you approach retirement and your reliance on that income diminishes, disability coverage becomes less important. Between the ages of forty to around sixty, however, it's worth considering.

HEALTH INSURANCE

The Affordable Care Act of 2010 (the ACA, or "Obamacare" for short) brought big changes to the *health insurance* landscape.

The ACA fundamentally altered the way health insurance policies are structured, sold, and administered in the United States. Whole books have been written about its effects, but for people nearing retirement, one point stands out: *Every American under age sixty-five must, by law, have health insurance.*

If you're retiring early, the ACA means you must buy health insurance yourself and maintain coverage until you become eligible for Medicare at age sixty-five. It can be a huge expense—remember Gary in chapter 2?

One of the ACA's positives was the creation of health insurance "marketplaces," where people could comparison-shop for coverage. That raised general awareness of the costs of health insurance and perhaps created more transparency in the industry.

But a downside also developed. The flood of people buying insurance in order to meet the ACA's requirement that everyone be insured—including the sick—caused insurer profitability to plummet, thanks to big jumps in health-care claims. That has prompted carriers to increase premiums or to drop out of the insurance marketplaces altogether.

It is a confusing time in the health-care insurance industry, but one thing is clear, and it's vitally important to early retirees—health insurance premiums are on the rise. In just one year, the top five companies in my home state of Minnesota increased rates for the same coverage between 14 and 49 percent, according to the Minneapolis *Star-Tribune.*

Imagine you're going to retire at sixty and buy health insurance for five years and that your premiums are going to increase 25 percent, year over year, until you become eligible for Medicare. Your insurance bill would more than double.

The key to buying insurance is to know what you need, but how in the world do we plan for *this*? It becomes very difficult.

INCOME-RELATED MEDICARE PART B PREMIUMS					
2016 premium projections based on 2014 MAGI					
	Income thresholds				
Single	<$85K	$85K-$107K	$107K-$160K	$214K	>$214K
Married	<$170K	$170K-$214K	$214K $320K	$320K-$428K	>$428K
2015	$104.90	$146.90	$209.80	$272.70	$335.70
2016- Held harmless	$104.90				
2016- Not held harmless	$159.30	223.00	318.60	414.20	509.80
Premium level	Standard premium	1.4 x Standard Premium	2.0 x Standard premium	2.6 x Standard premium	3.2 x Standard premium

Sources: Centers for Medicare and Medicaid Services as compiled by the Centers for Reitrement Research at Boston College.

I'd like to cite a statistic giving you an idea of the average cost of health insurance, but things are so dynamic right now that any such number will very likely be meaningless before the ink on this page has dried. If you are determined to retire early, however, here are two suggestions.

First, get a quote on health insurance right away, and watch the premium trends as you near retirement. Along with that trend, consider how various inflation rates might impact your cash flow between retiring and becoming eligible for Medicare at age sixty-five.

Second, decide how much coverage you'll need to fill that gap, based on how your own health is trending and your family's medical history.

If you anticipate a lot of medical needs, a "gold"-type policy is more appropriate. If you are fortunate enough to enjoy good health—not too many trips to the doctor yourself and few major illnesses among your ancestors—consider a "silver" or "bronze" plan. These offer less coverage and may have a higher deductible but will save you money. Just be aware that you are also playing the probability of not needing much care before you reach age sixty-five.

MORE ABOUT MEDICARE

We've covered *disability* and *healthcare*, two of the four types of insurance we're looking at in this chapter. Before we move on to *long-term care* and *life* policies for your later years, I want to spend a few moments on Medicare. You become eligible for this federal insurance program at age sixty-five.

Medicare is an across-the board system. If you are sixty-five, you get it, period. The basic benefits are identical for everyone, and every retiree counts on it for medical coverage.

Lyndon Johnson signed Medicare into law in 1965, adding a health-care component to the Social Security program Franklin D. Roosevelt had created thirty years before. Some people think going on Medicare "automatically" triggers Social Security retirement benefits, but that's not the case. You can claim Social Security retirement benefits at age sixty-two or seventy or any age between, but you'll be enrolled in Medicare at age sixty-five whether you've claimed Social Security or not.

A lot of myths and misconceptions surround Medicare. Probably the biggest is that Medicare is 100 percent free. That's true of the basic benefit (part A)—for most people. If you have a ten-year work history, then you probably qualify, and your nonworking spouse will too.

Though such cases are rare, a few people age sixty-five and older have not amassed enough working credit to qualify for Medicare Part A at no cost. They can claim based on their spouse's earnings history if still married (or widowed), but if they are single, they must purchase it. Rates, while lower than policies through private insurers, can still reach $400 per month (as of this writing).

Part A covers hospital costs, within limits. Since Medicare's creation, other parts have been added as the health-care landscape has changed. Those parts are not free, and the next one, Part B, is also *not optional*. So you *will pay* for Medicare—one way or another.

Part B helps cover doctor bills, outpatient care, emergency room visits, testing and other lab services, and certain medical equipment. As of this writing in 2016, the monthly payment is around $122 for most people. It is paid via automatic draft an account you designate. If you've already claimed Social Security, it comes straight out of your Social Security check.

This chart breaks out the cost of Part B for people at various income levels (again, these are 2016 figures).

Next to consider is Medicare Part C, an option providing sup-plementary coverage.

Also known as Medicare Advantage, Part C essentially adds coverage while expanding your health-care provider network—much like an HMO or PPO-type plan. About half of Medicare recipients buy Part C coverage, at an average additional monthly cost of around

$35 in 2016, according to the National Council on Aging. The cost can range up to $200 more, depending on the options selected.

Finally, there's Medicare Part D, which helps cover the cost of prescription drugs. Optional like Part C, Part D ranged between $10 and $100 per month in 2016 and carried a maximum deductible of $360 per year.

In terms of your retirement plan, deductibles, limits, and co-pays are really the whole key to Medicare. It's a worthwhile and valuable program, but none of its parts cover 100 percent of everything, particularly if you become very sick.

A good example: Part A fully covers only your first sixty days in a hospital. After that, you incur co-pays: $322 per day for days 61–90, and $644 per day beyond that (again, at 2016 rates).

Clearly, Medicare is not free, nor does it cover everything along the way. We must plan for that, but how? Medical expenses are hard to predict, and that's putting it mildly.

Fortunately, there is an insurance solution: supplemental coverage. Popularly known as "Medigap" plans, these policies are specifically tailored for folks over age sixty-five to—as the name suggests—fill the "gaps" in their Medicare coverage. For many people, they are an affordable solution to the risk of serious illness, which increases as we get older.

Medigap plans allow you to choose coverage appropriate to your general health, your financial situation, and your family medical history.

However you incorporate health-care coverage and possible medical expenses into your retirement plan, the following chart really drives home the importance of doing so:

Estimated median health care costs per person

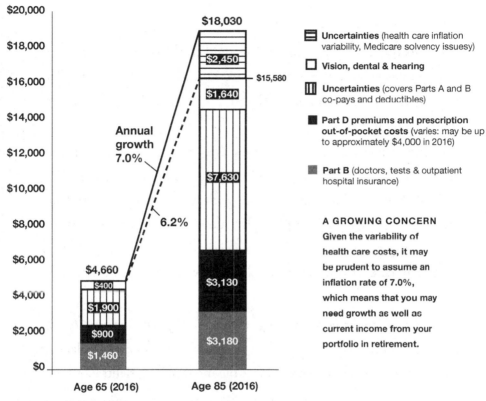

Source: Employee Benefit Research Institute (EBRI) data as of December 31, 2015;
SelectQuote data as of December 31, 2015; J.P. Morgan analysis.

Produced by Morgan Stanley Asset Management, the chart applies a factor of 7 percent per year to demonstrate the possible impact of increases to Medicare and Medigap coverage and to the cost of vision, hearing, and dental care across a twenty-year retirement. Needless to say, it's far better to overestimate than underestimate your costs.

I believe health-care coverage and the cost of unreimbursed expenses for medical care, combined, are the biggest hurdle most retirees will face along the way. Be sure to plan for them—and to get the help you need to do it right.

LONG-TERM CARE INSURANCE

"What if I wind up in a nursing home?"

This question is why most of us tend to think of long-term care insurance first, among the policies we consider for retirement. The real benefit of such coverage is that it can actually help you stay *out* of a nursing home.

The insurance industry defines *long-term care* as personal or custodial care that assists people with the activities of daily living (ADLs). These include eating, bathing, dressing, using the restroom, and moving from place to place. If a doctor determines that you're unable to perform two of these five activities, then you qualify for long-term care. If you experience a cognitive impairment, that alone is enough to qualify.

So, you might be wondering, *what's the difference between health-care insurance and long-term care insurance?* It seems you could be laid up awhile in either case and therefore face big medical bills, right? Not really.

Medical issues covered by health insurance—things requiring doctor visits, trips to the ER, hospitalization, drug therapy, and the like—carry a good chance that you will recover your health and get back to your ADLs. Long-term care insurance covers what—in all probability—will be a permanent loss of your ability to perform ADLs *on your own*. You're going to require long-term help.

That help may include skilled care by nurses, therapists, or physicians or less-intensive assistance from a qualified health aide. These services aren't necessarily provided in one facility. The health aide might visit your home to cook a meal or help you bathe. You might get physical therapy in an assisted-living or a senior-care facility. A doctor's care might occur in a full-fledged nursing facility.

Insurance underwriters carefully classify the types of care and the settings in which they might occur. They come up with odds, based on trends in the general population, on whether you will need one or more of these levels of care and on where the services are most likely to be provided. The underwriters then weigh the odds by the cost of services in your area, your general health, and your age when quoting the policy. Their findings determine the cost of your long-term care insurance.

When these policies were first being written back in the early 1980s, they were inexpensive compared to today. The insurance industry was just not ready for the big increases we've seen in life expectancies.

People say we're living in an age of medical miracles. The gains in life expectancy in the last thirty to forty years really prove it and are why, as we've seen throughout this book, people are spending longer in retirement than ever before.

For insurance companies, long life expectancies are a potential drain on profits. Insurers are paying out millions to cover the long-term care of baby boomers. To recoup those costs, they're charging much higher premiums on long-term care policies than when these policies were introduced.

How much do long-term care policies cost? I hope you're sitting down.

A couple fifty-five to sixty years old could pay in a range of $2,000 to $3,500 per spouse, *per year.*

Now, let's figure both spouses are sixty years old, both live to age eighty-five, and both are paying $2,500 per year. That's twenty-five years at $5,000, or $125,000. If the couple invested that money and got just a 5 percent annual return—are you ready?—$238,000.

You're thinking, *That's a big portion of my IRA!* You're right. You might also be wondering, *Do I really need long-term care insurance?*

The facts say yes, you do—or at least a *viable strategy* for covering the costs of long-term care. The following chart shows why.

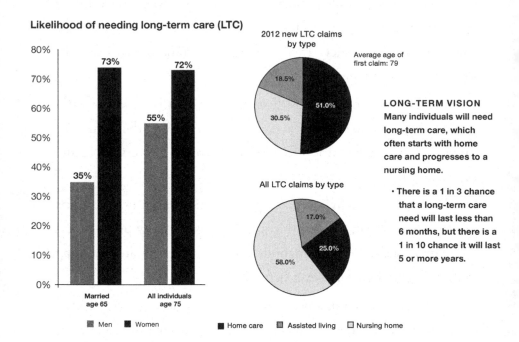

Likelihood of needing long-term care (LTC)

2012 new LTC claims by type

Average age of first claim: 79

LONG-TERM VISION
Many individuals will need long-term care, which often starts with home care and progresses to a nursing home.

• There is a 1 in 3 chance that a long-term care need will last less than 6 months, but there is a 1 in 10 chance it will last 5 or more years.

All LTC claims by type

Home care   Assisted living   Nursing home

Among married couples where both partners have reached age sixty-five, 73 percent of women will need long-term care at some point. The number is also significant for men, a better than one-in-three chance.

Maybe you're a single man and you like those odds. Okay, but look what happens when you go to all people (married or not) who reach age seventy-five. Still nearly three-quarters of women, but now *more than half* of all men, will one day require such care.

We're back to the big question: How do you afford this? I ask clients to look at three things when we're working on this part of their financial plan.

First, how much control do you want over the type of long-term care you will receive, if and when you need it? A policy (or planning strategy) that allows for a home health aide or for care in a nicer assisted-living facility might be important to some people but not as crucial for others.

Second, might long-term care insurance fill a dual role, providing not only care but acting as "inheritance insurance" for your family? If a goal is to pass assets on to loved ones, friends, or a charity, then that could influence the coverage you buy.

Finally we look at cost, and we do it in terms of the stress-testing we've been talking about throughout this book. How much cost can you absorb to buy a policy? Can you afford coverage at all?

I've done hundreds of financial plans for retirement over the years. Everyone's situation is different, of course, but whether to buy long-term care insurance and how robust a policy to purchase usually depends on the income clients need in retirement and on what assets they hope to pass along to their heirs.

Let's say you're a married couple. One spouse has $30,000 of annual pension income. Another $40,000 of Social Security benefits is coming in, between you, per year. That's $70,000 of income. You also have approximately $1 million in other assets, and you're living comfortably in retirement, without having to draw on them.

Imagine one of you becomes cognitively impaired and enters long-term care, a nursing home, or an assisted-living facility for three to five years. That could really change the dynamics. You could erode or even exhaust the assets in your estate.

This group—I'll call it the middle to upper-middle income group—really has the most exposure and the greatest risk if they opt to roll the dice and decide not to buy a long-term care policy.

For those with more significant assets, it becomes easier to say, "You know what? I'm fine. I have enough to pay for this, I really don't need a long-term care policy. I can insure myself."

Those on the lower end of the income spectrum might need to roll the dice too, if your cash flow is not enough to afford a policy.

With this in mind, the main questions middle-income earners need to answer while stress-testing long-term care options are:

1. What kind of care is important to me/us?

2. Are there assets we want to pass along?

The answers could determine whether you need coverage at all. If you decide that you do, that other question remains: How do you afford it? Luckily, like any type of insurance coverage, long-term care offers all sorts of options.

One strategy is to consider whether you can absorb a year or two of the expense of long-term care if a spouse winds up in a facility. Many middle-income retirees can, though if it goes much beyond that, the expense can really drain their assets.

One of the variables that underwriters apply when quoting long-term care policies is what's called an *elimination period*. It begins on the date you are deemed eligible for long-term care benefits. The effect of the elimination period is like the deductible on your car insurance: the longer the elimination period, the lower your premium.

Let's say most long-term care policies have an elimination period of sixty days, meaning you'll pay for the first two months of care out of your pocket. On day sixty-one, the policy would start paying whatever daily or monthly amount is stipulated. But what if we extend the elimination period—to a year, for instance?

That should reduce the cost of your policy, just like increasing the deductible on your car insurance does. You agree to cover costs up to a given amount, then the insurance takes over. This can protect you from your biggest worry, incurring costs for long-term care that are too high to comfortably absorb.

In short, you're protecting your assets, and that's what insurance is all about. We'd all love to have top-flight care, fully paid from day one, no questions asked. But distinguishing what you want from what you need is the key to spending wisely, whether we're talking about insurance or anything else. This strategy offers a potentially more-affordable solution to purchasing long-term care insurance with no elimination period, while also considering the possibility that care becomes necessary for an extended period.

LIFE INSURANCE

"In this world nothing can be said to be certain, except death and taxes."

You guessed it, Ben Franklin. This might be his best-known quote. We tackled taxes a couple of chapters ago, but now that we're into insurance—guess what?

When my planning sessions with clients come around to life insurance, I always ask a simple question: What is the policy you own today truly accomplishing for you? Some people can't really answer. They say, "I just figured I should have some."

While that probably makes the insurance industry very happy, I view things a little differently.

If something you own or invest in, particularly by the time you've retired, is not helping you to avoid debt and/or protecting you from a potential loss of income—or from the erosion of the assets that you have accumulated over the course of your lifetime—then you really need to assess that product's value.

It's easy to justify life insurance when we're younger: "If the worst happens, I want to provide for my wife and my kids." That makes perfect sense. We want our families protected because, early in our careers, we're in the asset accumulation stage. We're building a base that will support us in retirement and perhaps create a legacy for the next generation.

But if you're a couple of years from retirement, you've established that base. Your kids are grown and accumulating assets of their own. Perhaps you've paid off your house. If not, the payments are hopefully much lower relative to your income than when you were younger. Your spouse probably isn't as dependent on your earned income as before.

In short, you're in that "practicing for retirement" stage I've already mentioned, tailoring your lifestyle to match the income you'll have when you've come home from work for the last time.

I actually make the case that many retirees don't need life insurance at all. It's not protecting or insulating you from anything, and the premiums could just keep going up the older you get, for obvious reasons.

That said, there are also many reasons to own a life insurance policy. Two instances where I think life insurance can be of value later in life include covering the loss of a spouse who has a pension and simplifying estate planning.

If you have a single-life pension that only pays out while you're living, you might want to buy some life insurance on yourself, over a period of time, to replace that pension for your surviving spouse. You might want to do so for Social Security income that the surviving spouse would otherwise lose, as well.

In estate planning, life insurance is one of the easiest ways to transfer wealth upon death. It's a "clean" transaction, it's tax-free, and it can happen very quickly, so it can be an effective tool. Those features help from an estate-tax perspective, too, which we'll cover fully in the next chapter. For now, let's briefly consider which type of life insurance makes the most sense.

There are two basic types, *term* and *permanent*.

Permanent life insurance is sometimes called "cash value." Research shows permanent life insurance is the most-sold type, but for many, it is not the appropriate solution. The idea behind permanent insurance seems reasonable: a portion of your premium buys the policy, and the rest is invested in order to produce "cash value," from which you can draw—eventually. But it typically takes seven to ten years of premium payments before there's enough cash value to draw on. That's because the lion's share of the early payments go to the insurance company, not to building the cash value. Granted, that value does accumulate over time because the money in your permanent insurance policy grows tax-deferred.

Because a lot can happen in seven to ten years, these policies are not for everyone. High-income earners are one group, in my view, who might want to consider one but only if they've already maxed out their 401(k)s, IRAs, and other tax-advantaged vehicles.

Secondly, permanent insurance is beneficial in estate planning because it avoids the unknown of when the insured would pass away. This is why this is the most common life insurance vehicle used for estate planning. *Term* insurance would only cover the selected period and *permanent* avoids that.

For most, *term* life insurance can be a much wiser option, Here's why.

Premiums for term insurance are paid across a given period of time—the policy's term—and if you die while the policy is in force, your selected beneficiaries get the death benefit.

Let's say you want $200,000 of coverage. You buy a ten-year term life policy at a cost of $200 a year. (These are not actual prices, but the relative costs accurately illustrate the reality.) You die in year five. The company pays the full $200,000 to your named beneficiary. Simple, right?

Contrast that with a permanent, or cash value, policy.

For starters, the premiums are typically higher. Let's use $1,000 a year.

That's $800 a year, if you instead bought term life insurance, that you could be investing elsewhere for immediate gains. No waiting for the cash value—of what is, after all, *your own money!*—to build. More important, you get the protection you need, which is why you purchase insurance in the first place. For many families, the reason for having the life insurance changes upon retirement.

The bottom line: I generally come down on the side of limiting life insurance as retirement nears, unless one or both of the two quite specific instances just covered are in play.

In this chapter we've covered four types of insurance products with varying degrees of value in retirement and seen that the key is to know what we truly need. Otherwise, we might wind up buying a policy we neither need nor want.

On to chapter 9, where we consider the legacy you wish to leave and the most effective tools for protecting your estate and passing it on.

CHAPTER 9

ESTATE PLANNING FOR PEACE OF MIND

"I never worry about action but only inaction."

—WINSTON CHURCHILL

Your chances of enjoying the retirement you envisioned back in chapter 2 improve in direct proportion to how comprehensively you've planned for your financial future, and how closely you follow your plan. I strongly recommend regularly assessing and adapting that plan to changing personal and economic circumstances with the help of a trusted advisor.

Doing so could allow you to exceed your goals. The wealth you build might outlive you, creating a legacy to pass along.

Such remaining wealth, in all its forms—brokerage, checking, and savings accounts; real estate; IRAs, 401(k)-type accounts—is what is legally called your "estate." If you don't take action to designate where these assets go after you die, then you could do a real disservice to your survivors, who will have the task of sorting things out.

In this final chapter, we study strategies for ensuring that your estate benefits the people, institutions, and causes you most care about.

FACING OUR MORTALITY

Though I have referred hundreds of families to estate planning attorneys, this area remains the one most procrastinated on. Maybe you did your first will after your children were born and perhaps a basic estate plan when you took your first vacation without them. But have you updated anything since?

If you're like most people, the answer is no, and there's no better time than when formulating your financial plan for retirement.

Putting together a plan for your estate is—both literally and figuratively—the last thing on your planning plate. It helps assure an enjoyable retirement, thanks to the knowledge that all your potential "loose ends" have been tied up.

More importantly, it's the right thing to do for your survivors.

You've probably heard the same horror stories as me. A son or daughter is named executor of their parents' estate and tries to administer their wishes, but because not everything was properly titled or designated, it costs them weeks or months of time and frustration.

Don't get me wrong. Who among us, given a choice between playing a round of golf or sitting in an attorney's office and sorting out our final wishes wouldn't prefer the first? (Maybe even if we've never held a golf club!)

But the vast majority of my clients agree. The incredible sense of relief that comes with getting their estate planning done is well worth it. They feel good knowing that they have made their final intentions clear and that their families won't face decisions that really shouldn't fall to them in the first place.

TWO POSSIBILITIES

What actually happens to your estate after you die depends almost entirely on properly documenting what you *want to happen*. If you haven't, your remaining wealth could become subject to probate, a legal process by which the courts oversee or administer the distribution of your assets.

It's no stretch to think of estate planning as an investment. Probate courts come with fees and expenses—charges that can reduce the total value of your estate when the court's work is done. Proper estate planning reduces the possibility of probate and so may eliminate those fees.

Estate planning, therefore, is really about control. Without the documentation required to make your wishes known, the state could step in. If so, it will apply a set of standardized rules it has established for estate distribution—and the probate court's rulings might not match your wishes.

For example, you might have distant relatives, a life partner to whom you are not legally married, children from a previous marriage, a charity, or someone else you would like to receive some of your assets. If they are not legally classified as your closest next of kin, the probate court could ignore them.

"No worries," you're saying. "I have a will."

A will alone, however, does not avoid probate. Technically, in fact, it's the document that opens the door because it is public information. It is therefore open to challenge in court.

Your will is just an instruction manual, so to speak, describing what you want to happen. If you have not had it updated, however, or if it is not clearly written—and is challenged—then the court could interpret it in a way that runs counter to your intentions.

To maintain control over the distribution of your estate, there are a couple of key documents in addition to your will that can help: a *power of attorney* and a *health-care directive.*

A *power of attorney* (POA) helps clarify who you trust because it appoints someone to make financial decisions if you become unable to make them yourself. It could be as simple as paying your utility bills or as involved as discussing medical care invoices to ensure you are not overcharged during an extended hospitalization.

The POA entrusts your financial interests to someone who you are confident will go above and beyond to protect them on your behalf. That person's testimony can therefore carry serious weight if a probate court tries to interpret your intentions.

A *health-care directive* (sometimes called a *health-care declaration*) states your priorities and desires regarding health care, so providers know your wishes if you cannot communicate them. Do you want to be kept on life support? Do you want to be an organ donor? Do you want your body buried or cremated?

Both of these documents are typically prepared along with your will, and a clear, up-to-date will underpins both of them. A will also appoints an executor, the person charged with carrying out its intentions—often the same person named in your POA.

OPTIONS FOR TRANSFERRING YOUR ESTATE

Though your will designates a trusted person to speak on your behalf, the best protection against your estate landing in probate court is negating the possibility that it is challenged.

Being very specific about who gets what, within the will itself, is the surest way to achieve that, and there are three very good options for doing so: *gifting, joint ownership,* and *beneficiary designation.* The first two rely more closely on statements in your will; beneficiary designation is more automatic. Let's look at all three.

Gifting is just what it sounds like: giving assets to someone else. How and when you do so, however, can greatly impact the assets still at your disposal while you're living. Timing can also impact the tax burden for your gifts' recipients.

Say, for example, you begin gifting money while you're still alive, to help ensure that your estate is passed on to your family. As of 2016, you can gift $14,000 per year, per person, and your spouse can, too. If you give more than that to one person, then you must file a gift tax return. The federal lifetime exemption is $5,450,000 per gift-giver (again, as of 2016), so clearly, the tax code allows for significant gifting of assets.

What if you give stock instead of cash? Being a native Minnesotan, I'll again use 3M for this example.

Say that right now, today, you gifted me 3M stock with a *current* value of $14,000, but the *cost basis* on that stock—its value when *you purchased* it—was $7,000. When I receive that gift, I receive it at that basis value. Let's say I immediately sell it. I would pay capital gains tax on the $7,000 *difference* between its basis and current values because the IRS wants its take on the stock's appreciation.

Now let's say that, instead, you stipulated *in your will* that I'll *inherit* that stock when you die and that you died today. Doing that defers the taxes to me, but it works differently than it does with gifting. With inherited securities, the basis value is updated to their *current* value at the date of death, in this case $14,000. The $7,000 gain, the taxes on which I'd be liable, has been wiped out. That's a pretty profound difference.

A simple strategy then, when trying to transfer assets as tax efficiently as possible, is to let your *most-appreciated assets* be inherited, while gifting your least-appreciated ones, like cash. Doing so can help minimize taxes for both you and the recipient.

Something else to consider with gifting, of course, is that you lose the asset if you gift it while you're still living. What if you need it later?

Our second option, *joint ownership*, can help with that. Joint ownership helps keep your estate out of probate court by transferring assets directly to another person upon your death. Its technical name is "joint ownership with right of survivorship," but it's much simpler than it sounds.

Most couples pass assets from the deceased to the surviving spouse through joint ownership: simply titling assets in both their names. Assets held this way are transferred to the surviving spouse with the completion of a simple form or two. It really doesn't get much easier.

The third (and similarly simple) way of transferring your estate's assets is *beneficiary designation*. The most obvious example of this is listing beneficiaries for your IRA or 401(k)-type plan. You can do the same with life insurance and annuities.

For brokerage and bank accounts, the terminology is a little different. The mechanism is referred to as "transfer on death" (TOD), but the effect is the same. You're just designating the beneficiaries of those accounts.

In every case, the accounts are automatically transferred upon your death: no worries about winding up in probate court. It's clean and simple, and on most accounts, you have the option of naming contingent beneficiaries, one or more others who would receive the asset if the primary beneficiary passes before receiving the account. There are some distinct advantages in naming contingent beneficiaries, and I would encourage you to talk with a professional about what could apply to you.

Here's an important note: beneficiary designation typically overrides distribution directives concerning the same accounts included in another estate planning document—a trust.

"DO I NEED A TRUST?"

I get this question all the time. Some estate planning attorneys say everybody needs one, and probably an equal number believe it depends on your situation.

I tend to follow the latter group. Trusts can certainly benefit some people. In other cases however, it is quite unlikely that the scenarios that trusts are designed to address will play out.

Here's the better question to ask: Is the additional expense of setting up a trust worth it *for my situation?*

Trusts outline conditions and instructions for the distribution of *specific assets* within your estate, upon your death. A trust doesn't replace a will; it's typically done in addition to one. You don't have to be a Rockefeller or Warren Buffett to have a trust.

Trusts can be simple or complex, depending on your situation. I'm not going to delve into the legal ins and outs; this isn't a law school text, after all! What I will do is highlight a few reasons for trusts to help you decide whether exploring one makes sense.

Avoiding probate: If you want to keep your affairs out of the public eye, maintain control of your estate and avoid creditors, a trust may be right for you.

Limiting access to your estate: Do you have minor children or other beneficiaries whom you fear won't use your estate's assets wisely?

Not all children are irresponsible, but let's face it, receiving a large sum of money can have unexpected consequences, especially for those whose fiscal sense hasn't fully matured. A trust can help control the disbursement of your assets.

Avoiding estate taxes: The strategies around this are too numerous and complex to cover here, but ownership of real estate in more than one state is a big indicator that a trust might be prudent.

Discrepancies in real estate documents could land your estate in probate court. Since real estate isn't typically a liquid asset, titling multiple properties to a trust can help ensure they are transferred in a tax-efficient way, since tax rules vary from state to state.

Giving to, or establishing, a cause: A trust can designate a portion of your estate to—or even fund the startup of—an organization that advocates for issues important to you.

There are other reasons a trust may—or may not—be worthwhile. There are also different types of trusts: living and testamentary.

Living trusts are further broken down between "revocable" and "irrevocable." Testamentary trusts offer "pour-over provisions" that may or may not benefit you.

If you come to me to put together a financial plan, I can tell you pretty quickly whether a trust might make sense. But even if it does, I won't be the one setting it up. That's the job of an estate planning attorney—to discover, recommend, and implement.

I suggest working with an attorney where the first appointment is a free consultation. Get an understanding of how he or she operates, their fee structure and process. Make sure they're right for you. Any trust they prepare will be based on what you tell them and on the documentation you provide.

If you don't feel comfortable with this person, it can affect your confidence that your intentions will be fulfilled. Good professionals recognize this. They understand that the few nonbillable minutes required to establish a good working rapport with you is time well spent.

In this chapter, we've covered the basics of properly designating where the material wealth that survives you—your estate—ultimately goes. We've seen that the best reason to have an estate plan in place is selfish; it provides peace of mind.

Still, there's an altruistic element to estate planning. By clearly laying out your intentions, you help your surviving spouse, family, and friends simplify a task that, given its emotional nature, could otherwise be difficult, possibly even contentious.

Whether your estate plan is simple or complex, the relief of doing it correctly is worth it. Moreover, you'll set an example your loved ones will appreciate, and hopefully emulate, when their time comes.

As valuable and appreciated as the material things you pass along might be, passing the torch of responsibility by demonstrating the importance of estate planning might just be the greatest gift any of us can leave to those we care most about.

WHO DO YOU TRUST?

We've covered a lot of information in this book.

Needless to say, hard work goes into creating a financial plan tailored to your specific situation and goals, one flexible enough to adapt to an ever-changing economic climate.

As we learned in studying the work of the late Harvard psychologist David McClelland in chapter 1, the success of business owners and entrepreneurs is directly related to the depth and detail of their business plans. By planning for retirement with comparable rigor, you'll greatly increase the probability of overcoming your income gap.

Part of the planning comes by looking at what works, specifically at the habits of the wealthy. Besides the kind of stuff you'd expect— they have a good routine, they're very disciplined, they minimize risk—the wealthy that *stay* wealthy always have strong financial advisors that they can truly rely on.

That is not to say you really need to come work with me. But as we've also learned, there are a lot of people out there who simply push products, with little interest in their clients' success.

Whether the idea of composing, implementing, and regularly reviewing your financial plan for retirement seems doable or daunting to you, a trusted financial advisor—someone who will put your goals and needs first—will make it easier. I hope the expertise, concern, and level of detail provided in this book has convinced you that getting professional help is smart and has provided a model of the qualities you should seek in a trusted advisor.

This stuff is too complex—and far too important to your future—to go it alone or to risk working with anyone in whom you do not have complete confidence.

Thanks very much for reading. I bid you a happy, healthy retirement—one even better than you envision.

CPSIA information can be obtained
at www.ICGtesting.com
Printed in the USA
FSOW04n0529210117
29887FS